Challenging Stories

Challenging Stories

Exploring the Intersections between Health and the Humanities

E. THOMAS EWING AND
PRIYANKA GANGULY

VIRGINIA TECH
PUBLISHING

Copyright © 2024 Virginia Tech

Individual chapters copyright © 2024 respective authors

First published 2024 by Virginia Tech Publishing

Virginia Tech Publishing

University Libraries at Virginia Tech

560 Drillfield Drive

Blacksburg, VA, 24061

![CC BY-NC-ND]

This work is licensed under the Creative Commons Attribution-NonCommercial-NoDerivatives 4.0 International License. To view a copy of this license, visit https://creativecommons.org/licenses/by-nc-nd/4.0/?ref=chooser-v1 or send a letter to Creative Commons, PO Box 1866, Mountain View, CA, 94042, USA.

Note to users: This work may contain components (e.g., photographs, illustrations, or quotations) not covered by the license. Every effort has been made to identify these components, but ultimately it is your responsibility to independently evaluate the copyright status of any work or component part of a work you use, in light of your intended use.

ISBN: 978-1-962841-12-2 (print) | ISBN: 978-1-962841-13-9 (PDF) | ISBN: 978-1-962841-14-6 (EPUB) | DOI: doi.org/10.21061/challenging-stories

Front cover image: "Group of Medical Staff and Patients Outside a Building." Zwerdling Postcard Collection, 1900–1950, Images from the History of Medicine, National Library of Medicine, National Institutes of Health (NIH).

Contents

Preface   vii

Introduction   1
Challenging Stories
E. Thomas Ewing and Priyanka Ganguly

1. She Had No Marks of Violence Appearing on Her Body   9
   Enslaved Black Women in Virginia
   Kimberly V. Jones

2. The Indispensable Midwife   31
   Challenging the Narrative of the Rural Midwife in Twentieth Century New Mexico
   Gianna May Sanchez

3. La Grippe's Fearful Work   50
   Data and Narrative during the 1889–1892 Influenza in Alabama
   E. Thomas Ewing

4. Rethinking Techniques of Bleeding in Twentieth Century Iran   69
   Samin Rashidbeigi

5. Narrating Humor and Persuasion in Biological Safety Cartoons   86
   Chuan Hao (Alex) Chen

6. Population Growth and Mexico's Production of Family Planning Short Films   126
   Martha L. Espinosa

7. How We See Ourselves in History 146
   Stories of, by, and from Plant/People
   Macey Flood and Emily Beck

8. Making Vulnerable 164
   Exposure to Harm of Institutionalized Older Adults in Lima, Peru
   Magdalena Zegarra Chiappori

   Afterword 183
   Shared Horizons: Past, Present, and Future
   Jeffrey S. Reznick and Frank Vitale IV

   Contributors 193

Preface

This volume originated in a workshop funded by a National Endowment for the Humanities Chair's Grant for "Shared Horizons II: Data, Health, and the Digital Humanities" ($30,000). The workshop and this volume sought to uphold the remarkable commitment of Chair Shelly Lowe to support work in the humanities that addresses major challenges facing the nation and the world. Any views, findings, conclusions, or recommendations expressed in this book do not necessarily represent those of the National Endowment for the Humanities.

Three key figures were instrumental to the vision and outcomes of this project: Jennifer Serventi, Senior Program Officer in the Office of Digital Humanities; Jeffrey S. Reznick, Senior Historian, National Library of Medicine; and Peter Potter, Director Emeritus of Virginia Tech Publishing. Jennifer is a remarkable advocate for the digital humanities, whose commitment to broadening engagement and scholarship in this field was essential for the success of this project. Jeff's commitment to building connections between the digital humanities and medical history ensured that this project fulfilled the vision of the 2013 conference, *Shared Horizons*. Peter's vision for new approaches to scholarly publication, building upon advances in digital humanities and a commitment to open access, provide a model for scholarly work across fields.

At the National Library of Medicine, Sarah Eilers, Christie Moffatt, John Rees, and Krista Stracka contributed their archival and rare books expertise to discussions with workshop participants. Lindsay Franz and Kenneth M. Koyle, together with Edward Woodhouse and the National Institutes of Health (NIH) VideoCasting team, led the successful VideoCast and preservation of the online programs associated with the workshop. Elizabeth A. Mullen ensured the considerable amplification of these programs through the popular National Library of Medicine blog, *Circulating Now*.

This volume benefits from the efficient work and expert guidance of the staff of Virginia Tech Publishing: Peter Potter, Corinne Guimont, Jason Higgins, Emily Hills, Kindred Grey, Caitlin Bean, and Robert Browder. This book seeks to uphold and advance the commitment to new forms of open access publishing envisioned by Virginia Tech Publishing

At Virginia Tech, Amanda Pester, Laura Lawson, Amber Gilbert, Jessica Mills, and others from the Office of the Dean, College of Liberal Arts and Human Sciences, and the Office of Sponsored Programs provided essential administrative support.

The workshop participants were inspired by the scholarly insights and academic achievements of two keynote speakers: Kim Gallon, Associate Professor of Africana Studies at Brown University, and Kathleen Kole de Peralta, Clinical Associate Professor of Global History at Arizona State Universities. Their keynote addresses, broadcast and now archived by the National Library of Medicine, set an inspirational tone for the project, while their contributions to the workshop sessions challenged participants to think deeply about the connections between data, health, and the digital humanities.

Finally, and most importantly, this volume benefited from the scholarly community formed through the review of outlines, presentation of research materials, discussion of proposed revisions, and submission of numerous revisions. Alex, Emily, Frank, Gianna, Jeff, Kimberly, Macey, Magdalena, Martha, Priya, and Samin fulfilled the promise made in the proposal to organize a workshop that supported early career scholars, produced outstanding scholarship, and engaged with important issues in data, health, and the digital humanities.

Introduction

Challenging Stories

E. THOMAS EWING AND PRIYANKA GANGULY

On May 24, 2020, the New York Times filled the entire front page of the day's issue with names of individuals who had died of COVID-19 in the previous three months. Names were followed by hometowns, ages, and brief phrases that reflected the person's life. The issue marked the milestone of 100,000 deaths from this disease, which the headline called "An Incalculable Loss." More names filled out subsequent pages of the newspaper. The online version allows a viewer to scroll through days; watch the number of deaths accumulate; and pause to read names, ages, locations, and brief summaries of lives. The editorial comment accompanying this remarkable display of loss explored the meaning of counting deaths and mourning lives: "A number is an imperfect measure when applied to the human condition. A number provides an answer to how many, but it can never convey the individual arcs of life, the 100,000 ways of greeting the morning and saying good night" (Barry et al. 2020).

COVID-19 forced us to think about challenging stories both in our own individual lives and in the collective experience of our communities, regions, nations, and the world. Each victim in the New York Times list had a story, yet the collective stories of all the victims were a challenge to policy makers, health officials, and all of society. The New York Times visualized these stories, and our own experiences recreated that visualization in the minutes, hours, days, weeks, months, and years that became the accumulated experience of the pandemic.

The trajectory of this edited volume intersected with the experience of the pandemic in ways that shaped the purpose, content, and outcome. As discussed in the Afterword, the antecedent to this project, *Shared Horizons*, was a workshop hosted by the University of Maryland at College Park in spring 2013. The format of this event followed decades-old conventions of academic conferences and workshops, with participants traveling to the site, meeting in conference rooms, gathering for meals, and even (uniquely) attending a dinner hosted at the Library of Congress.

At the time, few could have anticipated how much the COVID-19 pandemic would disrupt the sense of what was "normal" for academic workshops. The pandemic, combined with technological advances facilitating video conferencing for multiple participants, disrupted the sense of place, connection, and participation embedded in traditional academic conferences. When we resumed planning for *Shared Horizons II* in the summer of 2020, we did not know how long the pandemic would last (and certainly underestimated its devastating effects in the years to come), but we knew that we could plan for a different format to achieve the goal of building a collaborative experience for workshop participants.

The themes of the workshop—data, health, and the digital humanities—remained the same, yet the venue changed to an all-virtual workshop, designed to facilitate sustained conversation among contributing authors. The two keynote speakers presented virtually to workshop participants, as well as hundreds of viewers around the world, as part of the History of Medicine speaker series hosted by the National Library of Medicine. Working sessions with authors allowed for initial presentations, peer reviews of drafts, consultations with coeditors, and reviews of revised drafts, all done virtually through digital platforms. Following the lead of other humanities and academic organizations in the aftermath of the pandemic, this workshop sought participation from early-career scholars, including advanced graduate students and recently completed doctoral recipients, with the goal of creating opportunities for these individuals to participate in a scholarly community. The eight chapters included in this volume emerged from this context, yet the research transcends the boundaries of COVID-19 in terms of the trajectory of the researchers and the themes, topics, and methods of these scholars. The workshop and edited volume had their origins during COVID-19, but are not directly about COVID-19, except to the extent that almost everything that has happened since 2020 has meant contending with COVID-19 in some form.

    These chapters bring together unique perspectives on challenging stories at the intersection of health and humanities. Kimberly V. Jones's chapter introduces an alternative perspective for understanding enslaved women's oppression through the lens of both white women's dominant authority and men's sexual perversion. This perspective confirms that the framework of challenging stories can advance understanding of important historical questions; the history of slavery should be unraveled by highlighting the experience of mothers, the meaning of disability, and the underlying power structures of the system of exploitation. Gianna May Sanchez problematizes the history of midwives in New Mexico by delineating how legislation and public health initiatives in the twentieth century shaped lay midwife practices. In addition, May Sanchez's chapter brings a different perspective of healthcare workers who challenged the dominant biomedical system and responded to patients who preferred midwifery care in their times of need. E. Thomas Ewing examines challenging stories as a global pandemic shapes the regional experience of illness, death, and loss in Alabama. Exploring the tension between quantitative analysis and qualitative interpretation, this chapter explores the presence and absence of measurements of racial disparities in health outcomes. Samin Rashidbeigi's chapter offers fascinating evidence and analysis about the ways that Iranians understood traditional ways of losing blood in the era before transfusions became common medical practice. These bloodletting and self-flagellation activities constitute a prehistory of the practice of bleeding that coexisted in tension with, rather than displaced, modern transfusion practices and tools. Chuan Hao (Alex) Chen's chapter showcases how a military safety office used texts and illustrations to persuade recalcitrant biological weapon scientists to change their attitudes and practices related to lab safety. A close reading of these illustrations in the American postwar context reveals how that strategy promoted a form of masculine hegemony in the form of gendered depictions. Martha L. Espinosa's chapter uniquely blends theoretical approaches to reproductive health policy with narratives featured in short films produced by the Mexican government to expose how the national narrative of modernization and development shaped messages and outcomes of policies and practices. The chapter coauthored by Macey Flood and Emily Beck brings an alternative history of herbalism (plant-related health practices) that challenges our views of monolithic and static concepts of plants, space, and culture. Through the oral histories with so-called plant people, the authors showcase how storytelling has been adopted as a rhetorical tactic for surviving and challenging dominant biomedical systems. Magdalena Zegarra Chiappori's chapter further broadens the idea of challenging stories by problematizing the notion of vulnerability in the tensions between the experiences of ungrievable populations, the professional location of healthcare workers, and the analytical position of the researcher.

The concept of *stories* encompasses a range of ways that the accounts of individuals provide perspectives on broader structural and social dynamics. Each chapter tells stories, yet the production of the chapters, in terms of research completed by each scholar, as well as in the collaborative nature of the workshop and editing process, also involves complicated stories of individual efforts and collaborative production. The word *challenging* was selected for the volume title because of the dual meaning of the word in its most common forms. As an adjective, challenging can mean demanding, difficult, or exacting, but as a verb, the word can also mean confronting, defying, or competing. Embedded in the book's title, therefore, is a tension between challenging stories, that is, stories of exacting or difficult circumstances related to diseases, medicine, and health, but also challenging stories, those that question the narrative format as a way to explain and experience disease, medicine, and health.

The photograph on the cover of the book was taken about a century before the *New York Times* commemorated the first 100,000 deaths from the COVID-19 pandemic (Zwerdling 1900–1950). At first glance, the photograph seems completely different in composition and character. More than fifty people sit or stand on steps of a building, all of them looking directly at the camera, with some of those in the back peering around those in front of them to make sure their faces are visible. Some individuals appear to be medical personnel, as indicated by the Red Cross armbands or uniforms suggesting physicians or nurses. At least ten of the medical personnel appear to be nurses, while the only man obviously in a medical uniform stands in the very center of the photograph, smoking a cigarette. Some men have bandages around their heads or splints for their arms, while others wear coats over clothing appropriate for hospital patients. Finally, the photograph includes some people dressed in office clothing, several who might be janitorial or housekeeping staff, and a few children. The caption associated with this item from the National Library of Medicine offers only a general date (1900 to 1950?) and the suggestion of a location (Bulgaria?). This version of the photograph was published on a postcard, 9×14 cm in dimensions, part of the Zwerdling collection of medical postcards, which means that the artifact itself is actually smaller than the reproduction of that image when viewed on a laptop or monitor screen.

This postcard photograph and the *New York Times* stand in opposite positions regarding the identity of individuals, as the completely anonymous (at least in the archival collection) women, men, and children in the photograph stand in sharp contrast to the precise name, date of death, and age of each victim published by the *New York Times*. We know that what is missing in each source in fact exists but is not part of the source: the physical presence of individuals rendered visible by the photograph conceals the fact that each person also had a name, an age, and a date of death, while the precise information published by the *New York Times* does not capture in any way the actual physicality of these 100,000 victims. These dualities of collective and individual identity are central themes of this volume, as the stories told by and about people in challenging contexts always involve this tension between unique experiences and collective processes. Just as the name, location, date of death, and keywords suggest the entire life story of 100,000 victims of COVID-19, the faces, clothing, and positions of these fifty women, men, and children on hospital steps suggest collective stories involving challenges from the past, present, and future from whatever starting date was the moment that this picture was taken.

The photograph of patients and medical personnel and the *New York Times* list of names also provide a reminder that context matters when thinking about stories. As noted above, the photograph of the hospital steps includes only a broad date range: 1900–1950. In fact, the clothing of the participants and more specifically the type of bandages suggest that we are looking at a military hospital, with the doctor and nurses caring for wounded soldiers in the First World War. While photographs of military hospitals are widely available from this era, Bulgaria's experience in the war was distinctive. Initially neutral when the war began in 1914, Bulgaria joined the alliance with Germany, Austro-Hungary, and the Ottoman Empire in 1915, fought against Russian forces in 1916 and 1917, and then collapsed as foreign armies invaded, troops mutinied, and the government fell as the war ended in 1918 (Hall 2011). This photograph captures a moment in time that came before, during, or after a period broadly characterized by loss, mourning, and disruption across this region.

The chronology of the *New York Times* list of names is more precise. Late May 2020 marked ten weeks after Americans began experiencing the extraordinary public health measures taken to control the pandemic, such as closing schools, limiting travel, and enforcing mask mandates. At a time when vaccines seemed as much as a year or more in the future, the trajectory of the disease appeared very unpredictable, with the 100,000 deaths listed in this issue thought to be just the beginning of a devastating epidemic. One week after this issue, George Floyd was murdered by a police officer in Minneapolis, setting in motion a national and indeed global movement to address racial inequities and structural racism (Nurridin, Mooney, and White 2020). The pandemic, and especially the public health response, and the movement for racial justice became the backdrop for an extremely divisive election that culminated in the assault on the Capitol on January 6, 2021. At the one-year anniversary of the start of the pandemic, in March 2021, the *New York Times* noted that more than half a million Americans had died from coronavirus, with a daily death rate of nearly 1,500 at a time when vaccines were only just becoming widely available (Leatherby 2021).

The chapters in this volume integrate two contrasting representations of individuals and their challenging stories. These chapters tell the stories of individuals, real people including historical figures and anonymized human subjects, in many cases in greater detail than is the case in either the newspaper list or the archival photograph. Yet each chapter also recognizes that the stories about individuals make sense only as a way to think about the stories of all the individuals who do not appear in these chapters. Just as the 100,000 deaths commemorated in May 2020 were only one-tenth of the more than one million victims in the United States, the individuals who appear in these chapters matter for who they are and for what they represent. We may not know their names, ages, or traits, as summarized in the *New York Times*, and we do not see their faces, as in the hospital photograph, but their stories provide the illustration that we need to understand their lives and why they mattered. The challenges posed by their stories are challenges for scholars to interpret and readers to understand.

References

Barry, Dan, Larry Buchanan, Clinton Cargill, Annie Daniel, Alain Delaquérière, Lazaro Gamio, Gabriel Gianordoli, et al. 2020. "An Incalculable Loss." *New York Times*, May 24.

Hall, Richard C. 2011. "Bulgaria in the First World War." *Historian* 73 (2): 300–15.

Leatherby, Lauren. 2021. "Despite Encouraging Downward Trend, U.S. Covid Deaths Remain High." *New York Times*, March 13.

Nurridin, Ayah, Graham Mooney, and Alexandre I. R. White. 2020. "Reckoning with Histories of Medical Racism and Violence in the USA." *Lancet* 396 (October): 949–51.

Zwerdling, Michael. 1900–1950. "Group of Medical Staff and Patients Outside a Building." Zwerdling Postcard Collection, Images from the History of Medicine, National Library of Medicine.

1. She Had No Marks of Violence Appearing on Her Body

Enslaved Black Women in Virginia

KIMBERLY V. JONES

In 1831, Milly, an enslaved woman from Isle of Wight County, Virginia, died from a diseased womb.[1] The affliction, which would later be known as cancer of the cervix uteri, could cause hemorrhaging, discharge, loss of muscles, weakness, and pain (Macnaughton-Jones 1894). Milly's death record in the Coroner Inquisition Record of Virginia erases the pain that likely preceded her death yet reveals the importance of enslaved women's reproductive labor. The condition of enslaved women's wombs—uterus, cervix, and fallopian tubes—was one component of their reproductive apparatus that required enslavers' attention. The death of a childbearing enslaved woman was a notable event for the loss of labor and laborers it represented. Some days after Milly's enslaver encountered her lifeless form, the coroner's jury arrived to determine "when, where, how, and after what manner" Milly "came to her death" (Coroner's Inquisition 1831). On her death, Milly, according to the coroners, "had no marks of violence appearing on her body." Historian Stephen Berry argues that nineteenth century county-appointed coroners sometimes acted more as "detectives than medical examiner" (Berry 2020). Milly's coroners' efforts to perceive the medical cause of her death ignored the traumas of

---

1. Enslaved women's wombs, their uteri, cervices, and fallopian tubes, were the vessels through which new generations of laborers were born.

slavery on her body and the critical causalities of her death. The reports obfuscated slavery as the primary cause that paved the way toward Black and enslaved people's deaths. Ultimately the "marks of violence" caused by enslavement are evidenced in conditions such as diseased womb, but the line coroners drew stopped within the bodies of the deceased, leaving slavery's violence unacknowledged.

Only through opening Milly's body did the jurors find that she died of a diseased womb. The twenty-four gentlemen freeholders "lawfully given" the "charge touching the death of Milly" did not think it necessary to record interviews with those in Milly's direct community to give meaning to her archival entry beyond notice of her death (Coroner's Inquisition 1831). Testimony about Milly's children or the person or persons who discovered her death is absent. As historians, including Jennifer Morgan (2021) and Jessica Marie Johnson (2020), have stated, the archives can inflict their own sort of institutional violence upon the narratives of Black life that require excavation.

The literature available on slavery and pregnancy describes the historical moments where the demands on enslaved women's reproductive labor intensified due to enslavers' need for enslaved women's reproductive labor to sustain the system of slavery (Morgan 2011a; Schwartz 2010; Turner 2017; Paugh 2017). Jenifer Barclay holds that "enslaved women's reproductive capacity was crucial to the maintenance of slavery" (Barclay 2021, 17). Barclay's text focuses on the constructions of disability and Blackness as both embodied experiences in slavery that rendered Black people unfit for freedom and citizenship under the veil of white supremacy. Sasha Turner points out that enslaved women's bodies were "important sites of political struggles" over the economy, slavery, and abolition (Turner 2017). Considering the necessity of slave labor reveals the developing ideologies of disability in connection to enslaved women's reproductive labor.

This essay exhumes histories of Black enslaved women's bodies through the silent stories from the Coroner's Inquisition Records of Virginia. Milly's death and the deaths of other women in the

Coroner's archives challenge the data on slavery's violence. Despite the importance of Black women's bodies in maintaining the institution of slavery and securing individual enslavers' financial solvency, the records left about Milly as a full person beyond the condition of her body remain obfuscated. In this way, the archive's construction reenacts the violence of slavery through institutional erasure. Enslaved women and their torment were critical to the system of slavery. The medical trauma experienced by enslaved women engaged in compulsory productive and reproductive labor was produced by the conditions of slavery. The coroner's record about Milly and other Black and enslaved women was brief, but the violence hidden from the eyes of jurors reverberates in the records of slavery.

If and when enslaved women's (re)productive labor ended in their death, white male members of their enslavers' community decided the language in the only record of their existence. The brief entry was often the final written record of their lives. Jurors held beliefs about Black women's bodies that often blinded them to the violence that slavery produced on women's bodies. Jurors marshaled a well of knowledge from early explorers' encounters with Africans; travelers to Africa produced a pseudoscientific theory about Black women's bodies and character. They argued that Black women were promiscuous, bruitish, and insensitive to pain (Seth 2018; Paugh 2017; Turner 2017). Enslavers employed these ideas in their methods of labor extraction while Black women bore the errors of emerging scientific ideas in and on their bodies in life and death despite the omissions in the reports.

Enslaved women's reproductive labor placed them at perpetual risk for the disabilities associated with sex, birth, and birthing. Black mothers attempted to mitigate their risks in the drama of childbirth by deliberately and clandestinely employing strategies to control their reproductive health.[1] Reproductive autonomy presented enslaved women with opportunities for resistance despite the trauma and violence that often accompanied their refusals. In the seventeenth century, colonial authorities attributed low birth rates in African captives on Black women's refusal (Morgan 2011a; Seth 2018). Though seemingly resolved in later centuries, this underveiling view of the duress that pregnancy, birth, and slavery caused seemed to inspire surveillance over Black women's reproductive labor. Sasha Turner evinces physicians' role in the surveillance of enslaved women's births (Turner 2017). They were intended to aid in the childbirth as well as ensure that enslaved mothers did not commit infanticide. When coroner jurors arrived to ascertain the cause of death of a child after a birth or miscarriage, they searched for evidence that enslaved women used "criminal agents" to induce abortion and examined a child's body for wounds and trauma consistent with infanticide (Nunley 2023). Enslavers could use evidence of abortion and infanticide to criminalize Black mothers and argue that they were lacking in maternal care (Seth 2018).

Productive and Reproductive Labor

Fanny and Lucy, two enslaved women in Virginia, were convicted for infanticide in 1852. The women lived in different Virginia counties, yet they shared indictment for causing the death of their children "feloniously, wilfully [sic] and of her malice" (Fore 1852; Terrel 1853). The lines stating that she "came to her death as a result of choking by her mother" is only a sliver of the full story (Coroner's Inquisition 1832). Coroner records fail to record the full story of enslaved mothers' reproductive labor and the trauma wielded by the institution of slavery. However, enslaved women's bodies remained critical to the system of slavery. Enslavers remained vigilant to the risks presumed in enslaved women's (re)productive labor from medical trauma and the risks to their authority if Black women gained full autonomy over their (re)productive labor. The conditions of slavery brought about such trauma.

Pregnant enslaved women could simultaneously represent good fortune for the potential for new human property and vexation for the temporary loss of productive labor. In 1807, a Frederick County, Virginia, enslaver petitioned the court about the disabled condition of an unnamed enslaved man and woman he hired for service from their primary enslaver (Shepherd 1807). The petitioner requested a favorable judgment for his decision to pay only five of the twelve months of hire for their labor because they did not work as needed for seven months of the year. The enslaved woman's disability that prevented her from laboring as the man desired was pregnancy. She had just recently given birth and was not expected to have another child because "she did not breed in such a manner." However, the unnamed enslaved woman became pregnant while under the hiring contract (Shepherd 1807). The enslaver evaded discussing who impregnated the woman; however, she did not contract the same disease as the male hired alongside her at the time. Several plausible explanations are present for the father of her child, one of which was the possibility that the petitioner fathered her child. Whatever the truth of her pregnancy, the hirer believed he was misled and made to bear the cost of care for a pregnant slave while the slaveholder was paid for her expected labor and the bonus of a future increase in his human property. The petition demonstrates enslavers' interest in enslaved women's bodies because they could produce and reproduce, as well as the fact that their long-term gains from reproductive labor entailed short-term losses of productive labor.

Beyond their capacity to perform productive labor, pregnancy, childbirth, and sexual labor could lead to short- and long-term disabilities for enslaved women. Women experience disabilities recognized today as gestational diabetes, acid reflux, severe morning sickness, bladder and urinary tract infections, migraines, preeclampsia, high blood pressure, depression, anxiety, tooth loss, and miscarriage. Additionally, childbirth itself could lead to infertility from a difficult birth. Pregnancy and the pressure on women's bodies from birthing were not the only cause of temporary or permanent disability for enslaved women. They could also experience persistent pain that accompanied the violence of their enslavement. As one physician observed: "Owing to the distention of the muscles during pregnancy, very considerable pain is sometimes felt" in women's pelvis, bladder, vulva, and urethra (Burns 1820, 11). Sex and sexual labor caused some enslaved women to suffer with venereal diseases that rendered them incapable of adequately performing more acts of sexual labor and reproductive labor (Savitt 1981; Fett 2002; Cooper Owens 2017). Enslaved women's (re)productive labor and evidence of venereal disease were essential considerations in their value even as these same considerations contributed to their deaths.

Doctors as well as coroner's juries regularly attributed deaths to women's reproductive organs. The cause of death related to the enslaved position of Black women as people and property. This duality was evident in the assertion that illness and injury connected with enslaved women's wombs, "exercise increases the patient's sufferings, and frequently, a walk is the determining cause of hemorrhage" (Coroner's Inquisition 1831; Lisfranc 1839). Enslavers' desire to maintain Black women as laborers and labor producers was at risk by the very nature of slavery as the demand for labor challenged enslavers' ability to safeguard the labor capacity of their human property.

Enslaved women with Milly's social position faced demands for productive labor and reproductive labor of their bodies. In practice, the same physical activity that allegedly caused her death was an unavoidable feature of productive and reproductive labor. Enslaved women were responsible for cultivation of crops, domestic labor such as cooking and cleaning, mothering children—enslaved and white—and sexual labor. As historian Jennifer Morgan noted, enslavers frequently described African women's fecundity alongside their productive labor capacity. Enslavers ascertained through false racialized beliefs that African women experienced easy childbirth and thus could "easily perform hard labor in the Americas at the same time" (Morgan 2011b, 36). Enslaved women were viewed as bodies that were suitable for hard labor, which made their experiences of childbirth filled with risk for disability. Enslavers "welcomed the birth of a slave," as historian Marie Schwartz notes; however, they disdained the loss of labor the event represented and as a result few employed the advice from agricultural journals to reduce the work assignments of pregnant enslaved women (Schwartz 2010, 127–28). Many white enslavers exoticized Black bodies and entered forced or coerced intimate relationships with enslaved people (Johnson 2020; Mitchell 2020; Morgan 2011a, 2021; Cooper Owens 2017; Roberts 1998). All forms of labor required that women's bodies be active. Pregnant enslaved women continued their expected productive labor, which could put them at additional risk during birth. Enslaved women were valuable and enslavers looked for solutions so that their human property could continue to perform all expected activities. At times, the treatment was worse than the cure.

One common affliction was uterine tumors. The fibroids that grow on the walls of the uterus of women could become cancerous. Doctors debated the appropriateness of applying iodine or mercury to the offending tumors. Universally, the use of leeches was believed to be "very beneficial" because "it encourages the bleeding, and relaxes the parts, and by these means removes the excessive pain which is usually present" ("Traité Theoretique" 1847). In 1841, Susan, an enslaved woman in Prince Edward County, died at the age of sixty after having complained of being unwell (Coroner's Inquisition 1841). She was given the "usual attendance and medicine" but "did no business." Uterine ailments could prove agonizingly painful and Susan's enslaver's allowance for her respite speaks to the frequency and severity of medical conditions that necessitated care for women's reproductive ailments. Perhaps leeches or mercury were used as they were common treatments in the nineteenth century. Leeches' saliva may produce painkilling effects in patients, but mercury use could damage the nervous system and lead to long-term and chronic health challenges (Hohmann et al. 2018; Leake 1757). Controlled use of iodine could reduce cancerous cells;

however, improper dosage can cause adverse reactions in patients. Doctors viewed their treatments as applicable, and in some measure, they could prove effective; however, the nascent phase of medical treatment meant that all applications held a substantial amount of risk, and this risk was frequently borne by enslaved women (Leake 1757; Cartwright 1828; Haymart et al. 2011). Through Susan, we understand that afflictions such as the one she complained of were common enough to produce a standard of care that was discussed and tested. Still the usual medicine could often do as much damage as the illness itself (Mitchell 2021).

Susan's enslavers' insistence that she "did no business" does not represent the full story of the labor that elderly Black enslaved women performed (Coroner's Inquisition 1841). Slave retirement was only expressed in the distance from field labor (Kulikoff 2012). By the nineteenth century, aged enslaved people acted increasingly as nursemaids to old or infirm enslavers. Some older slaves continued their labor in fields while others were relegated to labor in enslavers' homes—as cooks, servants, nannies, or maids—depending on the level of investment in the domestic slave trade by enslavers. In addition to physical labor, elderly slaves worked as mentors to the different labor positions and attempted to acclimate people to slavery. Enslavers used older slaves often in the organization of slave labor (Close 1992). At the age of sixty, Susan's body was accustomed to the constant toil of slavery. In death, her enslavers found her in the kitchen, where she likely slept as well as worked. Such a position granted her no freedom between work and rest. The coroner's jury examined Susan's body and found marks and wounds that according to them likely occurred due to convulsions. According to the men tasked with viewing her body, death "did not come by means of any violence" (Coroner's Inquisition 1841). As she succumbed to death, Susan incurred more marks of slavery's violence at the end of her life. The ultimate cause of her death was noted as "a falling of the womb" but it was slavery that directly produced the conditions for her death (Coroner's Inquisition 1841). As was the case with Milly, who died a decade before Susan, death was the result of years of productive and reproductive labor compounded by medical neglect and mistreatment.

Black women were viewed positively for their potential to add to the labor regimes of slavery and subsequently the wealth of the enslaver. Enslavers' financial interests were accompanied with varying degrees of fascination and distaste for the distinctiveness of their skin and features that separated them from normative whiteness (Morgan 2011b). The duality that existed between distaste and desire infected medical practice. Physicians believed Black patients to be universally unworthy of painless treatment. Their unworthiness stemmed from the insistence on Black incompatibility to pain; instead, the pain that Black women experienced in reproductive labor was intensified due to the medical treatment intended to secure their wombs' value for enslavers. This disregard was compounded by the fact that Black women's pain helped determine the care that white women experienced. The techniques and procedures in gynecology that were performed through the trauma Black women experienced served as the basis for this medical field (Cooper Owens 2017). Surgery was required to alleviate the symptoms of a diseased womb, which was a remedy that could be harmful to the health of enslaved women. The disregard for the pain for enslaved Black women was confirmed by the statement from the coroner's jurors that Milly "had no marks of violence appearing on her body." An autopsy was needed to determine the cause of death, yet the absence of marks ignores the very reality of slavery that left Milly marked by violence. From the nature of slavery's violence to the potential treatment she could have received from medical professionals, violence marked the lives and bodies of enslaved Black women, even if these marks were made invisible by the structures of slavery and medicine who performed (re)productive labor.

Law, Labor, and Trauma

Enslaved women were cognizant and fearful of the value placed on their sexual labor in slave markets. Racial science portrayed Black women as hypersexual and claimed that their "inherent promiscuity made them more prone to venereal disease" (Willoughby 2022). Bethany Veney, known as Aunt Betty, employed a strategy that exploited enslavers' fears of acquiring a slave disabled due to a sexually transmitted infection. She did so by bending their desire to secure enslaved women for sexual labor for her own purposes. When displayed at the slave market, Aunt Betty was unresponsive and exhibited a feverish countenance and tongue (Veney 1889). Her performance was constructed out of sight of a watchful jailer. Alongside Aunt Betty, a "young slave girl," named Eliza was adorned by a dressmaker to "attract the attention of all present, if not in one way, [then] in another" (Veney 1889). Garbed in gaudy attire, the women were presented to potential owners and physicians to check their disability for the purposes of labor and desirability for sexual exploitation. Enslavers and speculators on the slave market viewed women with interest in their productive, reproductive, and sexual labor. A physician's role was to not only examine the potential property for evidence of physical, (re)productive, or sexual disability but to examine slaves for signs that they feigned illness such as that which Aunt Betty performed in resistance to slavery. Virginia enslavers sometimes placed troublesome slaves on the slave market to rid themselves of the threat from their resistance (Perrin 1844; Gudmestad 2003; Deyle 2006). As punishment, an enslaved person could be marked or disabled, and those were signs physicians looked for on the slave market. Some slave-owners feared after the Nat Turner Revolt in 1831 that they would purchase a future insurrectionist. A visible physical disability or scarring could indicate evidence of punishment and thus a predilection for resistance. In addition, scarring could accompany sexually transmitted diseases. Still, enslaved women's potential to extract themselves from the worst abuses of slavery was always fraught with danger because the system necessitated their trauma and short-term disability.

The force of law, labor, and trauma that twisted enslaved women's lives would also contort their bodies and minds. The disturbing incidents of rape caused enslaved women pain. Wendy Warren writes about the rape of an enslaved woman and the agonizing and heart-wrenching aftermath that lingered in the archives if not the moment (Warren 2007). Incidents of rape caused prolonged mental turmoil and afflicted enslaved women's bodies with greater risk of complicated pregnancies and sexually transmitted diseases (Keckley 1868; Jacobs 1861). Added to the turmoil of the act was the inability to protect oneself from violence and the heavy penalty for doing so. Flora, an enslaved woman in Frederick County, Virginia, murdered a man after she had argued with and struck his wife in 1808. Flora allegedly told the enslavers' wife that "she had long owed him a spite, that he was always going at her like a dog at an opossum that she intended to kill him and was ready to be hanged tomorrow for doing so" (Coroner's Inquisition 1808). Flora's argument could have stemmed from unwanted sexual attention and the censure that she experienced from the man's wife.

The archives suggest some enslaved women used enslavers' licentiousness for their own purposes. The question of enslaved women's ability to claim agency of their reproductive labor by securing and massaging sexual interest of their enslavers leads to questions of consent (Cooper Owens 2017). Women in the nineteenth century did not hold authority over their sexual labor no matter their race. For enslaved women, the discourse around their promiscuity heightened their vulnerability to sexual deviance (Morgan 2011b).[2] In the present, scholars and legal experts research

---

[2]. Interest in the nuances of consent is increasingly attended to in an era in the contemporary narrative about the #MeToo movement and newly constructed legal definitions of rape and sexual assault that account for power differences (Shaw 2022; Finley 2020).

the nuances of consent and explore how slavery rendered enslaved women incapable of denying sexual attention, as such slavery is an impairment that silences the victim (Sublette and Sublette 2015). Such considerations transform definitions of rape and sexual assault. Annette Gordon-Reed presents a more complicated relationship between consent and force in her study of the Hemingses of Monticello. At age fourteen, Sally Hemings acquiesced to the sexual advances of her enslaver and third President of the United States, Thomas Jefferson. Although Jefferson did not grant Hemings nor their children freedom until after his death, Hemings's sexual availability for Jefferson could have been a deciding factor in his posthumously granting her freedom. Gordon-Reed suggests that when Sally Hemings's family member, Madison Hemings, referred to her as a concubine, they were invoking norms both legal and cultural in Virginia about the relationship of an unmarried woman living with a man where the woman would act as a "substitute wife." Gordon-Reed suggests that one marker of white enslavers' intention and care for enslaved women was their treatment of children under the hindrance of laws that impacted enslavers' ability to fully acknowledge intimate relationships with Black women (Gordon-Reed 2008).

When Aunt Betty remarked that an enslaved woman would attract interest "if not in one way then another," she suggests that the young girl on the market with her, Eliza, was purchased for productive, reproductive, and sexual labor (Veney 1889). Betty, unlike Eliza, was able to escape momentarily to decide the direction of her labor by feigning disability on the slave market. For women who could not use a public performance to discourage interest, their route toward some measure of autonomy could resemble women such as Sally Hemings. Hemings as a youth appears to have been coerced into a sexual relationship that had potential to lead to freedom. Like other enslaved women, Hemings's so-called choice was mitigated through the powerlessness of the position as slave. In 1814, an enslaved woman, Milley, in Augusta County, endured the "criminally [unlawful] and carnally intimate" attentions from an enslaver whose wife was left in "total neglect and despair" and took great offense to the sexual interest Milley endured (Dunlap 1814). Milley likely bore children, fathered either by another enslaved man or, as the female enslaver suggests, by Milley's white male enslaver. Milley's body would be made to endure frequent pregnancy stemming from enslavers' economic desire for her (re)productive labor as well as his sexual interest, which transformed Milley into an object for multilayered desires and overlapping labor demands. Furthermore, the labor demands from enslavers pressed women such as Milley and their bodies into heightened service rendering them more vulnerable to disability. Enslaved women's reproductive labor, though valuable, could cause disabilities.

Enslavers formulated a strategy to account for pregnancy and to "make use" of enslaved women's reproductive possibilities. Scholars have argued that enslaved women's reproductive labor was understood through racializing Black women's bodies as the root of a duality of hypersexualization and asexual domestic labor (Schwartz 2010; Barclay 2017). Both labor roles allowed them to take advantage of the labor of enslaved women and continue practices and policies of extraction, however traumatic and violent to the victims of enslavers' desire for profits in slavery's capitalism.

As Milley's story emphasizes, the scrutiny Black enslaved women faced extended into relationships with white women as well (Dunlap 1814). Sexual violence and forced sexual labor experienced by Black enslaved women forced white women to consider their own ability to maintain financial authority. Such authority was often intimately tied to Black women's bodies. Milley's white woman enslaver sued for divorce from her husband due to his sexual relationship with Milley. The petitioner asked permission to keep her property, which included Milley and other enslaved people, and void the marriage. In making a claim to Milley's body and labor separate from the authority of her husband, the petitioner also asserted her raced and gendered position while turning Milley's sexual trauma into a reminder about forbidden sexual labor between white men and Black enslaved women.

The petitioner did not state Milley's intended fate, nor did she express Milley's thoughts or feelings about her relationship with the petitioner's husband. As property, Milley had no legal recourse to refuse violent or coercive labor, reproductive, productive, or sexual (Dunlap 1814). Her status compelled her to engage in disabling labor and denied her victimhood. Relationships between Black and white Virginians were under the legislature's scrutiny, but they were by no means uncommon. The petitioner's insistence that Milley's carnal intimacy with her husband was illegal stemmed from some of Virginia's earliest laws (Brown 1996; Wadlington 1966).

Enslavers often expected sexual labor from enslaved women; however, enslaved women were not always compliant. Fannie Berry describes how she directly challenged her enslavers' right to her body (Berry 1976). During her Works Progress Administration interview, conducted in 1937, Berry recounted the sexual trauma she endured as a slave in Virginia. Fannie Berry fought her enslaver when he threatened her with sexual violence. When he told her "What I can't do by fair means I'll do by foul," Fannie "scratched his face all to pieces" (Berry 1976). She ends the story with a poetic sigh, saying, "Us colored women had to go through plenty." Narratives told by formerly enslaved women reveal fragments of the forced pregnancies and mental trauma of rape in slavery. Although enslaved and free Black women were labeled promiscuous, they denied these claims in their actions and words.

The archives reveal the heavy burden of reproductive labor borne by enslaved women and the damage it caused their bodies even while some white physicians claimed ignorance of Black women's reproductive mortality. Although doctors in the nineteenth century worked to become the primary authority on the bodies of all people, they continued a practice of erasing any knowledge of the disabilities and pain enslaved women suffered through the demands of slavery. In 1881, Dr. T. Gaillard Thomas wrote that "it is a remarkable fact that negro women never have cancer of the uterus." According to Thomas and a colleague, in a "vast number of cases of ovarian cyst, I have never yet met a single instance of it in the negress" (Gaillard 1881). Thomas appeared unaware of the dozen Black women who died from diseases of the womb as recorded in the Coroner's Inquisition Records across the country. As a South Carolinian born in 1831 and educated in Charleston, Thomas would have gained experience from practicing on enslaved women's bodies at the South Carolina Medical College, which established a surgery specifically for the treatment of "negroes." The faculty enticed free Black people and enslavers into the hospital by promising to offer free medical advice from the first of November until the fifteenth of March (Nicoll 1903). Their stated objective was never philanthropic; instead, they declared the desire to collect as many exciting cases as possible for the benefit and instruction of their pupils. Faculty of the Medical College infirmary advertised to "buy up an assortment of damaged negroes, given over, as incurable, by others, and to make such . . . interesting cases, instead of experimenting on those who are the property of others" (Weld 1839, 171). Black and enslaved women suffering from falling wombs or a diseased womb would likely lay on examination tables, perhaps hoping for relief and finding pain instead (Smith and Willoughby 2021). Thomas's claim that "negro women" did not suffer ovarian cysts is particularly curious, considering his long training on Black women's bodies in South Carolina. Thomas seems willful in misrepresenting the possibilities of Black women's disabilities. Ovarian cysts were accompanied by pain and vaginal bleeding, which could render Black women unable to perform labor. The training developed and received by antebellum physicians was distorted by racialized notions of Black women's bodies and influenced the medical field for generations, as Black women continue to engage in battles for their bodily autonomy and medical freedom.

Black mothers labored in harsh conditions of slavery during their pregnancies. Enslaved women labored under the expectation that they could and would endure severe abdominal or pelvic pain during pregnancy, which was not uncommon and could hinder the labor they performed (Morgan 2011a). Frequent childbearing was a concomitant condition that made "falling wombs" common among enslaved women (Byrd and Clayton 2000). Falling of the womb occurred too frequently for enslaved women, according to enslavers (Collins 1803). Under such conditions, miscarriage, stillbirths, and postpartum ailments caused disabilities and disablement for enslaved women. According to the 2023 Equal Employment Opportunity Commission, the Americans with Disabilities Act does not consider pregnancy as a disability. However, this document acknowledges that pregnant workers will have impairments related to their pregnancy that may render them disabled for an abbreviated period and further states that employers must provide reasonable accommodation for people with pregnancy related disablements (Byrd and Clayton 2000). Based on the descriptions available about enslaved women's deaths, when their reproductive labor organs were compromised, the demands continued for their productive labor, which left them more vulnerable to disabilities and death. When they faced the turmoil of a traumatic birth, it was often followed by the real and immediate threat of separation from their young children. According to the accounts, their disabilities impacted their ability to perform the physical labor expected of them as slaves and the reproductive labor expected of them as enslaved women—and they were expected to remain stoic in the face of familial separations. Enslavers disputed the appearance of pregnant enslaved women on slave markets due to the belief in their diminished capacity for labor even while they held the future value of slavery in their wombs.

Conclusion

The enslaved women in slaveholding households experienced gender-specific ailments and gynecological disablement due to their reproductive and productive labor hardships. Enslaved pregnant women endured ailments that could render their productive labor inefficient. Digestive ailments could make eating difficult and cause nausea. Pregnant women frequently faced mobility difficulties. The ailments would necessitate concessions for pregnant enslaved women's level of productive labor. At the same time, enslavers bragged about their human property's ability to reproduce despite pregnant enslaved women's diminished productive ability. The coroner's record obscures the violence that disabled enslaved women through their reproductive labor. Enslaved women's labor expectations around reproductive labor placed them at perpetual risk for the disabilities associated with sex, carrying a child in their womb, and birthing. Milly, who begins the chapter, and the other women who animate the narrative likely died from an inability to rest from their continued expectations of production and reproduction. They died of slavery.

References

Barclay, Jenifer L. 2017. "Bad Breeders and Monstrosities: Racializing Childlessness and Congenital Disabilities in Slavery and Freedom." *Slavery & Abolition* 38 (2): 287–302.

Barclay, Jenifer L. 2021. *The Mark of Slavery: Disability, Race, and Gender in Antebellum America*. Urbana: University of Illinois Press.

Berry, Fannie. 1976. Interview published in *Weevils in the Wheat: Interviews with Virginia Ex-Slaves*. Charlottesville, VA: University of Virginia Press.

Berry, Stephen. 2020. "Database of Coroners' Inquisitions Taken Over the Bodies of Enslaved, Formerly Enslaved, and Free Black Peoples in the U.S. South, 1840s–1890s." *Journal of Slavery and Data Preservation* 1 (2): 10–14.

Brown, Kathleen M. 1996. *Good Wives, Nasty Wenches, and Anxious Patriarchs: Gender, Race, and Power in Colonial Virginia*. Chapel Hill, NC: University of North Carolina Press.

Burns, John. 1820. *The Principles of Midwifery: Including the Diseases of Women and Children*. London: Longman, Hurst, Rees, Orme, and Brown.

Byrd, W. Michael, and Linda A. Clayton. 2000. *An American Health Dilemma: A Medical History of African Americans and the Problem of Race; Beginnings to 1900*. New York, NY: Routledge.

Cartwright, Samuel A. 1828. "Cartwright on Iodine and Hydriodate of Potash." *American Medical Recorder* 15 (2): 257–89.

Close, Stacey Kevin. 1992. "Elderly Slaves of the Plantation South: Somewhere between Heaven and Earth." PhD dissertation, Ohio State University.

Collins, Date. 1803. *Practical Rules for the Management and Medical Treatment of Negro Slaves in the Sugar Colonies*. London: J. Barfield.

Cooper Owens, Deirdre. 2017. *Medical Bondage: Race, Gender, and the Origins of American Gynecology*. Athens, GA: University of Georgia Press.

Coroner's Inquisition. 1808. "Flora: Coroner's Inquisition Frederick County, Virginia." Frederick County, August 25. *Virginia Untold: The African American Narrative*, Virginiamemory.com.

Coroner's Inquisition. 1831. Isle of Wight County Virginia. *Virginia Untold: The African American Narrative*, Virginiamemory.com.

Coroner's Inquisition. 1832. "Fanny: Coroner's Inquisition Albemarle County, Virginia." Albemarle County, July 21. *Virginia Untold: The African American Narrative*, Virginiamemory.com.

Coroner's Inquisition. 1841. "Susan: Coroner's Inquisition Prince Edward County, Virginia." Prince Edward County, April 23. *Virginia Untold: The African American Narrative*, Virginiamemory.com.

Deyle, Steven. 2006. *Carry Me Back: The Domestic Slave Trade in American Life*. New York, NY: Oxford University Press.

Dunlap, Ellen Shields. 1814. "Petition to Augusta County, Virginia against Robert Dunlap for Divorce Naming Milley, an Enslaved Woman, as Mistress to Her Husband." University of North Carolina at Greensboro, October 12. Race and Slavery Petitions Project, Series 2 County Court Petitions, Accession 11681419.

Fett, Sharla. 2002. *Working Cures: Healing, Health, and Power on Southern Slave Plantations*. Chapel Hill, NC: University of North Carolina Press.

Finley, Alexandra J. 2020. *An Intimate Economy: Enslaved Women, Work, and America's Domestic Slave Trade*. Chapel Hill, NC: University of North Carolina Press.

Fore, Judith. 1852. "Claim for 'Six Hundred and Fifty Dollars the Value of My Negro Girl Lucy Sentenced to Be Hung by the Hustings Court for Infanticide.' October the 9th 1852." *Virginia Untold: The African American Narrative*, November 1. Library of Virginia, Condemned slaves and free blacks executed or transported records, 1781-1865, Accession APA 756, box 8, folder 14, Richmond.

Gaillard, Edwin Samuel, ed. 1881. *Gaillard's Medical Journal and the American Medical Weekly*. Vol. 31. New York, NY: A.G. Sherwood.

Gordon-Reed, Annette. 2008. *The Hemingses of Monticello*. New York, NY: W. W. Norton.

Gudmestad, Robert H. 2003. *A Troublesome Commerce: The Transformation of the Interstate Slave Trade*. Baton Rouge, LA: Louisiana State University Press.

Haymart, Megan R., Mousumi Banerjee, Andrew K. Stewart, Ronald J. Koenig, John D. Birkmeyer, and Jennifer J. Griggs. 2011. "Use of Radioactive Iodine for Thyroid Cancer." *Journal of the American Medical Association* 306 (7): 721–728.

Hohmann, Christoph-Daniel, Rainer Stange, Nico Steckhan, Sibylle Robens, Thomas Ostermann, Arion Paetow, Andreas Michalsen. 2018. "The Effectiveness of Leech Therapy in Chronic Low Back Pain." *Deutsches Arzteblatt International* 115 (47): 785–92.

Jacobs, Harriet. 1861. *Incidents in the Life of a Slave Girl*. Boston, MA: Boston Stereotype Foundry.

Johnson, Jessica Marie. 2020. *Wicked Flesh: Black Women, Intimacy, and Freedom in the Atlantic World*. Philadelphia, PA: University of Pennsylvania Press.

Keckley, Elizabeth. 1868. *Behind the Scenes, or, Thirty years a Slave, and Four Years in the White House*. New York, NY: G. W. Carleton.

Kulikoff, Allan. 2012. *Tobacco and Slaves: The Development of Southern Cultures in the Chesapeake, 1680–1800*. Chapel Hill, NC: University of North Carolina Press.

Leake, John. 1757. *A Dissertation on the Properties and Efficacy of the Lisbon Diet-Drink a Medicine, for Many Years, Successfully Used in Portugal, in the Cure of the Venereal Disease and Scurvy. Together With Reflections on The Improper Use of Mercury*. London: Royal-Exchange; Cornhill; H. S. Cox

Lisfranc, M. Jacques. 1839. *Diseases of the Uterus: A Series of Clinical Lectures*. Boston, MA: W. D. Ticknor.

Macnaughton-Jones, Henry. 1894. *Practical Manual of Diseases of Women Uterine Therapeutics*. New York, NY: William Wood and Company.

Mitchell, Elise. 2021. "Unbelievable Suffering: Rethinking Feigned Illness in Slavery and the Slave Trade." In *Medicine and Healing in the Age of Slavery*, ed. Sean Morey Smith and Christopher Willoughby. Baton Rouge, LA: Louisiana State University Press, 99-120.

Mitchell, Robin. 2020. *Vénus Noire: Black Women and Colonial Fantasies in Nineteenth-Century France*. Athens, GA: University of Georgia Press.

Morgan, Jennifer L. 2011a. *Laboring Women: Reproduction and Gender in New World Slavery*. Philadelphia, PA: University of Pennsylvania Press.

Morgan, Jennifer L. 2011b. "'Some Could Suckle over Their Shoulder': Male Travelers, Female Bodies, and the Gendering of Racial Ideology," in *Laboring Women: Reproduction and Gender in New World Slavery*. Philadelphia, PA: University of Pennsylvania Press.

Morgan, Jennifer L. 2021. *Reckoning with Slavery: Gender, Kinship, and Capitalism in the Early Black Atlantic*. Durham, NC: Duke University Press.

Nicoll, Henry D. 1903. "The Late Dr. T. Gaillard Thomas," *Medical Record* 63 (26): 1015–17.

Nunley, Tamika. 2023. *The Demands of Justice: Enslaved Women, Capital Crime, and Clemency in Early Virginia*. Chapel Hill, NC: University of North Carolina Press.

Paugh, Katherine. 2017. *The Politics of Reproduction: Race, Medicine, and Fertility in the Age of Abolition*. Oxford: Oxford University Press.

Perrin, George H. 1844. "Petition to Harrison County, Kentucky to Sell Amy (35) an Enslaved Women Who Has Become Troublesome," July 25, Folder 20784410, Race, Slavery, and Free Blacks, Series II: Petitions to Southern County Courts, Part C: Virginia (1775–1867) and Kentucky (1790–1864).

Roberts, Dorothy. 1998. *Killing the Black Body: Race, Reproduction, and the Meaning of Liberty*. New York, NY: Vintage.

Savitt, Todd. 1981. *Medicine and Slavery: The Diseases and Health Care of Blacks in Antebellum Virginia*. Urbana, IL: University of Illinois Press.

Schwartz, Marie Jenkins. 2010. *Birthing a Slave: Motherhood and Medicine in the Antebellum South*. Cambridge, MA: Harvard University Press.

Seth, Suman. 2018. *Difference and Disease: Medicine, Race, and the Eighteenth-Century British Empire*. Cambridge: Cambridge University Press.

Shaw, Jenny. 2020. "In the Name of the Mother: The Story of Susannah Mingo, a Woman of Color in the Early English Atlantic." *The William and Mary Quarterly* 77 (2): 177–210.

Shepherd, Moses. 1807. "Petition to Frederick County Virginia Court against Drusilla Ball." University of North Carolina at Greensboro, March 5. Race and Slavery Petitions Project, Series 2 County Court Petitions, Accession 21680712.

Smith, Sean Morey, and Christopher Willoughby. 2021. *Medicine and Healing in the Age of Slavery*. Baton Rouge, LA: Louisiana State University Press.

Sublette, Ned, and Constance Sublette. 2015. *The American Slave Coast: A History of the Slave-Breeding Industry*. Chicago, IL: Lawrence Hill Books.

Terrell, Alexander, ed. "Claim for A. F. Terrell to Receive $650.00 for Fanny a Slave Condemned for Transportation from Albemarle in 1852." *Virginia Untold: The African American Narrative*, October 8, 1853. Library of Virginia, Condemned slaves and free blacks executed or transported records, 1781–1865, Accession APA 756, box 8, folder 15, Albemarle County.

"Traité Theoretique et Pratique d'Auscultation Obstetricale." 1847. Summary published in *Medico-Chirurgical Review* 6 (12): 495–506.

Turner, Sasha. 2017. *Contested Bodies: Pregnancy, Childrearing, and Slavery in Jamaica*. Philadelphia, PA: University of Pennsylvania Press.

Veney, Bethany. 1889. *The Narrative of Bethany Veney: A Slave Woman*. Worcester, MA: Home of Little Wanderers.

Wadlington, Walter. 1966. "The Loving Case: Virginia's Anti-Miscegenation Statute in Historical Perspective." *Virginia Law Review* 52 (7): 1189–223.

Warren, Wendy Anne. 2007. "'The Cause of Her Grief': The Rape of a Slave in Early New England." *Journal of American History* 93 (4): 1031–49.

Weld, Thomas Dwight. 1839. *American Slavery as It Is: Testimony of a Thousand Witnesses*. New York, NY: American Anti-Slavery Society.

Willoughby, Christopher. 2022. *Masters of Health: Racial Science and Slavery in U.S. Medical Schools*. Chapel Hill, NC: University North Carolina Press.

2. The Indispensable Midwife

Challenging the Narrative of the Rural Midwife in Twentieth Century New Mexico

GIANNA MAY SANCHEZ

In a 1954 newsletter about the state of public healthcare, the New Mexico Department of Public Health praised the work of public health nurses, lamenting the conditions they had to work in to improve infant and maternal health in the state.[1] The article emphasized the impoverished conditions of the rural areas of the state, the "hot, dust-choking bit of New Mexico wastelands" (New Mexico Department of Public Health 1954, 26). In this supposedly inhospitable region, access to medicine was limited. In the case of infant health, "almost 1,000 babies who are born [in New Mexico] without any 'professional assistance'" could only rely on the aid of family, neighbors, and lay midwives (New Mexico Department of Public Health 1954, 26). As historian Lena McQuade-Salzfass noted in her chapter on midwifery in New Mexico, midwives in particular were integral to maternal and infant health in the state and were an indispensable resource in rural New Mexico (McQuade-Salzfass 2014). These women were not trained at a university, yet their expertise, paired with a public health certification, validated their license to practice and affirmed their significance to public health officials. Beginning in the 1920s, the Department of Public Health offered courses to license these midwives, who were then able to continue their practice into the latter half of the twentieth century

---

1. At the time, Dr. Gerald R. Clark served as the director of the Department of Public Health. He served in this position from July 1953 to July 1955, before leaving to work at the Morristown State Hospital in Pennsylvania. The director of the Division of Maternal and Child Health was Dr. Alvina Looram, who also started her position in 1953 (Greenfield 1962).

(Ortiz 2005).[2] By 1954, approximately 230 midwives were registered with the Department of Public Health (New Mexico Department of Public Health 1954). These practitioners attended 1,020 deliveries, roughly 4.8 percent of all state-recorded births, which was slightly higher than the national average of 3.2 percent (Dunn 1956). However, this focus on midwives in the countryside overshadows their work in urban spaces as well. Rather than a rural phenomenon that resulted from a lack of other options, lay midwives were an integral part of maternal and infant health as a viable medical resource for women throughout New Mexico.

New Mexico's formal support of lay midwives in public health initiatives and legislation was distinct in an era when physicians and hospitals dominated the provision of maternal health and childbirth (Walzer Leavitt 1986). In the late nineteenth and early twentieth centuries, the profession of medicine in the United States increasingly set standards for its practice and directed the options for care available to pregnant women (Walzer Leavitt 1986). However, this transition occurred on a delayed timeline for New Mexico, and women maintained greater autonomy over their reproductive lives as midwives remained available to them. As one 1948 account attested, "Only an exceedingly small proportion of women consult the physician during pregnancy" (van der Eerden 1948, 10). Instead, women would turn to lay midwives and other folk practitioners, using their services alongside any available care provided by a licensed physician as they saw fit. As the Department of Public Health noted, "The midwife, as part of the drama of birth, has almost disappeared from the American scene, her job taken over by hospitals staffed with competent obstetricians and trained nurses. But not so in New Mexico. The lack of nearby physicians in remote areas of the state, coupled with certain ethnological

---

2. New Mexico did not establish the Department of Public Health as its own entity until 1937. Prior to this year, the department was known as the Bureau of Public Health, and operated under the jurisdiction of the State Board of Public Welfare. For clarity, this chapter refers to this organization as the "Department of Public Health."

customs, have in the past made La Partera [the midwife] indispensable. Instead of pushing the midwife totally aside, however, New Mexico made her an important part of public health activities" (New Mexico Department of Public Health 1954, 27).

This praise, rather than an unequivocal show of support for midwifery, was a main source of tension for public health officials. Instead of an indispensable facet of healthcare, in the early twentieth century, public health officials and medical professionals viewed New Mexico's reliance upon these women as an unfortunate concession in rural communities and a temporary solution to statewide limitations in healthcare. As this chapter argues, New Mexicans' sustained reliance upon lay midwives throughout both rural and urban spaces as birth attendants indicated a more complex reality of medical pluralism, individual choice in reproductive agency, and cultural praxis of Mexican American communities in the state. These conditions allowed for women to assert autonomy in obstetric care and reinforced a space for midwives to continue their work in spite of a shifting and professionalizing medical landscape.

The first part of this chapter will lay the groundwork for how midwives practiced medicine in the state, including how they derived their work from Mexican folk healing practices (*curanderismo*). Then, I will provide an overview of New Mexico's medical landscape as professionalization and modernization efforts in the late nineteenth and early twentieth centuries led to the development of new legislation to regulate medicine. While physicians in the state increasingly sought to restrict who could practice medicine, the state's infrastructure, medical inaccessibility, and economic limitations required them to allow the work of midwives to continue into the latter half of the twentieth century. The chapter concludes by countering public health and medical officials' assertion that the use of midwifery was a distinctly rural practice. Instead, digital mapping suggests an alternate reality wherein midwives were dispersed throughout the state, including in Albuquerque, its most populous city with the greatest concentration of physicians.

Midwifery and *Curanderismo*

"La Partera," as mentioned in the public health bulletin, specifically referred to Mexican-descended midwives that drew from *curanderismo*, or Mexican folk healing practices (Torres 2006). The Department of Public Health used *"partera"* and midwife interchangeably, though medical legislation and similar records referred to the same women as "lay midwives." This difference in terminology was likely to distinguish between medical professionals who received formal medical education at universities and midwives, who were trained through apprenticeships. Midwives themselves varied in how they identified and labeled their work. In one instance, Aurora Garcia, who was certified as a midwife in 1925, did not include her profession in the 1930 census record (Bureau of the Census 1930). Using census records and information from the Department of Public Health is an imperfect metric to know how someone like Aurora viewed their work within New Mexico's medical landscape. Furthermore, words like "folk healer," while technically synonymous with the type of "folk medicine" practiced by these midwives, encompass other medical epistemologies including Indigenous medical practices. Native American midwives in Pueblo, Navajo, Apache, and other Indigenous communities were practicing medicine throughout this period as well.

In the early twentieth century, however, the Department of Public Health viewed New Mexico's Indigenous population as a separate entity. The department did not include Native American communities in state statistical analysis until 1943. Instead, the Office of Indian Affairs handled much of the public health and medical regulations on reservations, including collecting population data (Anderson 1927). In the case of midwifery certification, the

Department of Public Health described the women that participated in the licensing process as Mexican- or Spanish-descended, so while Indigenous midwives technically could have attained certification through this program, public discourse about their work would not have identified them as Indigenous. According to Robert Trennert, Native American communities would have likely hesitated in participating in state health programs. His work focuses on the Navajo Nation, and he argues that many individuals on reservations distrusted Western medical practice and Anglo-American physicians, choosing instead to rely on their own healers and remedies (Trennert 1998). As such, Native American folk healers and lay midwives are not included in this chapter because any analysis that incorporates these histories alongside Mexican-descended midwives would be beyond the scope of this project.

This chapter focuses on Mexican-descended and Spanish-speaking communities in New Mexico. In general, categorization of race and ethnicity in New Mexico is messy and complex (Sánchez 1940). In archival records, public health officials and medical professionals tended to identify individuals living in rural towns as "Spanish American" or "Mexican," regardless of citizenship or personal preference. Elite Mexican-descended families often identified as "Hispano" or "Spanish American," in part as a way to distinguish themselves from lower-class counterparts (Mitchell 2005). In census data, families with Spanish surnames were likely to identify themselves as "white" because other options did not "fit" and claiming whiteness granted access to greater power and rights compared to "non white" counterparts (Holtby 2012, 159–61). For the purposes of this study, I use "Mexican-descended" or "Mexican American" to refer to lay midwives and their communities, unless otherwise noted. This terminology, while imperfect, acknowledges the cultural practice of *curanderismo* that midwives drew from as well as the racialized division reinforced by public health officials and medical professionals, who viewed New Mexico's folk healers and Spanish-speaking population as a racial and cultural "other."

New Mexico's Medical Landscape

By the early twentieth century, the national transition to using exclusively physicians for obstetric care was underway (Walzer Leavitt 1986). However, New Mexico lagged behind this trend, supporting the continued practice of midwifery in legislation and through a certification program from the Department of Public Health. This continued reliance was a consequence of the state's infrastructure and economic limitations as well as its cultural heritage. Physicians crowded in more populated towns along the railway, while the majority of the state's population remained out of reach in rural communities. Furthermore, poor road conditions rendered these towns inaccessible by car. When the secretary of the New Mexico Board of Health, Francis Atkins, wrote about these conditions in 1897, he noted that the majority of the state's population, whom he described as "Mexican peasants, Navajo and Pueblo Indians," were too difficult to access and would not have been interested in the services of licensed physicians (Atkins 1897). This assumption drew from racist perceptions of New Mexicans, marking them as inferior and "primitive," decidedly not of interest to physicians that settled in the state, and not included in an idealized Anglo American patient group. Meanwhile, the people discounted in Atkins's account would have been deterred from relying on physicians because of this attitude. Furthermore, physicians charged too much for their services and very few spoke Spanish or understood the cultural nuances of their patients. The need for midwives continued as a result of this convergence of factors.

Legislation was critical to enabling the continued practice of midwifery in the state. In 1880, a small community of eleven physicians formed the Las Vegas Medical Society (later renamed to the New Mexico Medical Society). Their primary focus was to define standards for regulating the practice of medicine in the state. In an effort to model national standards and to assert the legitimacy of New Mexico's medical community—which was in question as the country debated if the territory was "American" enough to attain statehood due to its Catholic, Mexican-descended population majority—the New Mexico Medical Society adapted legislation from Illinois to propose a Medical Practice Act (Mitchell 2005). According to one report following its passage, the bill "utilize[d] the best materials from kindred statutes throughout the United States," signaling the territory's desire to mirror US state legislation and be seen as an American entity (Otero 1899). Up until this point, the territory struggled in its bid for statehood because the United States viewed New Mexico as incompatible with a "modern" (i.e., white and Protestant) America (Holtby 2012). Physicians, along with legislators and other community leaders, sought to change this view through measures like the Medical Practice Act.

In spite of widespread recognition of the importance of defining and codifying medical standards, the legislation stalled before it could become law ("Legislative Chat" 1893). The state House initially approved the proposed bill in March 1892. However, territorial Governor Bradford Prince vetoed the Medical Practice Act in February 1893, one year later (Prince 1893). He cited the bill's limited capacity to address the medical needs of New Mexicans, particularly women. As he argued, the Medical Practice Act would limit the freedom of choice for patients to choose their medical practitioner, especially in rural communities. He emphasized how the bill's medical regulations would impact women's autonomy in childbirth: "A more serious oppression is considered by Section 8 [of the bill]. It is well known that in many parts of the territory the services of a mid-wife are all that are usually employed in cases of childbirth. . . . But the bill under consideration limits that by . . . [making it] illegal to employ a mid-wife whenever a doctor may be within possible reach" (Prince 1893).

The current state regulations at the time for medicine did not have any restrictions on midwifery and when a woman could consult one. With the new Medical Practice Act, utilizing a midwife when a physician could be within the vicinity would be illegal. As such, women would be required to choose physicians as their birth attendant, regardless of their ability to pay or personal preference. This restriction did not account for any personal objections to a particular physician, including if the patient preferred to use a female birthing attendant or needed someone fluent in Spanish. Prince did not explicitly mention language issues, but he did emphasize the importance of personal preference and economic limitations in choosing a medical practitioner, and he further criticized physicians' own "desire to fix a high standard for the medical profession in New Mexico ... [which] overlooked the present condition of the territory and the necessities of the people, especially in rural districts" (Prince 1893).

This veto of the Medical Practice Act surprised and enraged members of the New Mexico Medical Society ("Editorial Correspondence" 1893). It effectively halted the passage of the bill for two years until 1895, when the legislature proposed a new version. The revised regulations allowed women to choose their birth attendants and midwives to continue their work. Accordingly, the New Mexico Medical Society could not "prohibit gratuitous service in cases of emergency, or the domestic administration of family remedies, or women from practicing midwifery" (Otero 1899, 270). New Mexican physicians and government representatives strove to modernize the territory through medical regulation in line with national trends that emphasized the need for standardized education in medicine, with only a select few permitted to practice medicine based on these regulations. However, they could not bar midwives from the birthing room because of cultural, infrastructural, and economic limitations in the state.

The implementation of the Medical Practice Act further reflected the realities and limitations of professionalizing medicine in a territory dominated by an existing system of healthcare and network of folk healers that met the needs of their patients and shared a cultural background. It reinforced the work of midwives and the autonomy of women to direct their medical care. It was through this initial negotiation of medical legislation that folk healing and midwifery could continue, becoming a permanent fixture of New Mexico's medical landscape as it was codified in the state's laws. The work of midwives would continue "in the margins of medical practice," coexisting with physicians and other health practitioners as the twentieth century progressed (Armus and Gómez 2021, 4–8).

Midwife Consultant Program

Midwives continued their work in the background of maternal and infant health efforts in New Mexico following statehood in 1912. The Department of Public Health, bolstered by funds from the 1921 Sheppard-Towner Act, began to train lay midwives based on updated standards for obstetrical care. The Sheppard-Towner Act provided federal support for states to improve maternal and infant healthcare and to establish educational programs for public health (Meckel 1990). New Mexico made use of these funds by establishing the Midwife Consultant Program, which assigned two public health nurses to offer courses on public health and evaluate the work of practicing midwives across the state. The Department of Public Health emphasized that this continued reliance upon midwives was temporary at best, and training required midwives to refer patients to a physician, especially for difficult pregnancies (Scott 1944).

Although public health officials acknowledged the need for midwives, their work was still viewed as backward and subpar. Public health nurses assumed midwife negligence and ignorance, and lessons in the program emphasized the "importance of cleanliness, non-interference, recognition of abnormal conditions, use of silver nitrate . . . and filling out the birth certificate" ("Trained Midwives" 1921). Instructional materials depicted midwives not as competent medical practitioners but as substitutes for "proper" medical care. One newspaper account emphasized the necessity of lay midwives to improve infant health, while also condemning midwives that did not meet certain standards, labeling them as "dirty." The report noted how Sheppard-Towner funds were being used to "educate the better class of midwife and rule out those unable to come up to standards of cleanliness and intelligence" ("Trained Midwives" 1921). This emphasis on cleanliness and ignorance persisted throughout the program's operation, stemming from long-standing racist assumptions about "dirty Mexicans" (Mckiernan-González 2012).

Even as public health officials maintained this patronizing viewpoint, they had to concede that midwives were part of "a historical institution, bound up in the life of our native people. In the isolated rural community, [they are] all that is available in the way of obstetrical care" (Bureau of Public Health 1923). At the time, the state struggled with its infant and maternal health. In the 1920s and 1930s, New Mexico had the highest rate of infant mortality at approximately 140 per 1,000 live births, more than twice the national average, with only two other states that had rates higher than 100 deaths per 1,000 births (Whorton 2002). Sheppard-Towner funds were specifically allocated to address this issue, and the state channeled this resource into health education, nurses employed in public health, and the training of midwives. As an additional benefit, lay midwives could serve as an intermediary between the Department of Public Health and isolated, Mexican-descended communities. From birth certificates submitted by midwives, the state could access more accurate census data, and important public health information could be disseminated through midwives to their patients.

While the department would expand and redouble its efforts to certify and regulate midwifery in the 1930s, not all midwives in New Mexico participated in the Midwifery Consultant Program. In fact, the majority of midwives during the 1920s and 1930s did not have full licensure. In 1938 and 1939, 768 midwives delivered 7,553 babies in New Mexico. Less than one-third (214) of the midwives were certified. This lack of complete compliance with certification requirements could have been due to difficulties in accessing or completing coursework or due to a lack of seeing certification as necessary. Requirements for completion could be demanding; participants were required to attend ten courses on public health guidelines and midwifery, and certified midwives needed to pass a physical examination to verify their abilities. In one instance, the department barred a midwife in 1921 from practicing medicine due to blindness ("Trained Midwives" 1921). Midwives who completed the certification program also had to sign a pledge to embody "certain safeguards to their patients," working under state surveillance to ensure they were following proper protocol ("Trained Midwives" 1921). Even after certification, midwives would need to take courses in subsequent years and pass examinations to renew their license. In 1939, eighty midwives attended at least ten courses but failed to complete the full licensure requirements.

In spite of these hurdles, midwives who completed the coursework seemed to benefit from the program. The Department of Public Health emphasized the general willingness of participants, and "Sheppard-Towner nurses . . . [found] the midwives eager to learn the fundamentals of asepsis and the danger signs that call for medical attention" (Bureau of Public Health 1923). Most importantly, midwives who completed the program obtained state certification, enabling them to continue their work, albeit under the supervision of the Department of Public Health. In reflecting on her participation in the certification program, Jesusita Aragón expressed some relief in having easy access to physicians in difficult deliveries. In recollections of her work, she noted the ability to consult physicians and refer patients to hospitals if the need arose. In one case, an infant was born with organs outside of their body, and after discussing the matter with a physician and nurse, Aragón was able to have the baby airlifted to Albuquerque, where medical care at a hospital enabled the infant to survive (Aragón 1987). While limiting at times, midwife certification did provide resources to practitioners and built a network between physicians and midwives. It also offered an opportunity for midwives to establish their own community among themselves, building camaraderie through shared coursework and experiences.

Throughout the early twentieth century, midwives continued to attend deliveries in steady numbers. In 1929, midwives attended approximately 29 percent of all births in the state, with an even higher rate in rural counties. In 1936, one county in northeastern New Mexico reported a 72 percent rate for midwife-attended births. Even in areas with established maternal health clinics with a licensed physician available, the majority of patients still utilized midwives for deliveries (Scott 1944). Although the continued reliance on these women for obstetric and maternal health frustrated public health officials and medical professionals, the rates of midwife-attended births and the lack of alternative medical resources left authorities with few options but to allow the midwives to continue their work. In 1938, Hester B. Curtis, the director of the Division of Maternal and Child Health, wrote, "Until we can change time-honored folkways, and until we can provide telephone communications, swifter means of travel, more doctors and the funds with which to pay them, we shall continue to have midwives in rural New Mexico" (Department of Public Health 1938).

Challenging the Rural Divide

As Curtis emphasized in his report, the Department of Public Health viewed the consistent reliance on midwifery in the state to be a rural issue. In more populous towns like Albuquerque or Las Vegas, physicians were readily accessible, and, presumably, people did not have as great a need for midwives. In addition, the department attributed the ongoing issue with infant mortality to the lack of "proper" healthcare in these small towns (New Mexico Medical Society 1928). Public health officials and physicians alike viewed poor infant health as a consequence of insufficient education in childrearing for mothers and in obstetrics for midwives (Bureau of Public Health 1926). Accordingly, the department focused any effort to improve infant healthcare in the state on education, as seen in the use of Sheppard-Towner nurses to certify midwives. As one Sheppard-Towner nurse, Teresa McGowan, described her work, her goal was to "teach the midwives to be more careful in handling maternity cases, as well as to demonstrate to women in remote rural districts how to care for and nurse cases of sickness" (Bureau of Public Health 1923).

Statements by physicians similarly blamed a lack of education in rural areas on the high rate of infant mortality. As Dr. J. C. Kisner condescendingly remarked at the 1928 New Mexico Medical Society annual meeting, "In the rural districts I have been in places where the women did not even know how to give a baby a bath, or how to feed it" (Kisner 1928). This focus on rural New Mexico stemmed from racist perceptions of the majority Mexican-descended people that lived there. Just as Atkins distinguished between potential patients and "Mexican peasants, Navajo and Pueblo Indians" in 1897, so too did Kisner view the communities thought to be the cause of poor infant health in the state. The consensus between physicians that emphasized the connection between rural residence and ignorance, as well as the Department of Public Health's insistence that public health nurses and the education they provided were the best solution to improving infant health, stemmed from patronizing, racist rhetoric that dismissed infant mortality as the fault of rural communities.

Midwives were part of this condemnation. Degrading the intelligence of rural New Mexicans further served to benefit physicians because it provided an easy scapegoat to explain infant mortality and the poor health conditions of the state. In the same way, midwifery could continue to be viewed as an inadequate medical resource that would not be utilized if there was enough medical infrastructure in New Mexico. By dismissing infant mortality as an issue concentrated in rural areas of New Mexico, however, the accounts failed to acknowledge the presence of midwives outside these spaces, in towns that had access to licensed physicians. If midwives were able to practice in areas where physicians were readily available, their value to the community would be far greater than public health and medical officials were willing to acknowledge. In fact, the distribution of lay midwives and physicians across the state indicated as much. In 1925, one report recounted how a county health department representative, A. B. Courtney, led classes for three months to train midwives in Bernalillo County, including the towns of Chilili, Tijeras, Alameda, Ranchos de Atrisco, and San Jose. In total, thirty-seven midwives completed the program and were subsequently certified,[3] including at least ten that lived in Albuquerque, the most populous town in the state ("Midwives Given Licenses" 1925).

With a population of 26,570 by 1930 and an extensive network of physicians in comparison to the rest of the state, Albuquerque, by the Department of Public Health's and the New Mexico Medical Society's estimation, should have had no need for midwives (Bureau of the Census 1930). While an exact count of physicians in Bernalillo County is difficult to ascertain, in 1925 there were a total of 365 physicians practicing in the state (American Medical Association 1925). By 1928, there were thirty-nine physicians in Bernalillo County that were members of the New Mexico Medical Society, which likely reflected the total number of physicians practicing in that county at that time because physicians in the state held membership to the medical society in high regard (Cohenour 1928). Albuquerque consistently had one of the highest concentrations of physicians in the state during the twentieth century (Spidle 1986).

---

3. Their names are as follows: Nastacia Chavez, Aurora Garcia, Eugenia Shubert, Telles Gonzales, Marialita Garcia, and Isadora Trujillo of Alameda; Carolina Caldwell of San Antonito; Julianita Romero Trujillo of Frost; Roay Guest of Barton; Predicanda Gutierrez of Yrissari; Edwigen Mora of Escabosa; Librada Gutierrez and Severa Armenta of Chilili; Olimpia Garcia and Gregorita Herra of Carnuel; Paz Jaramillo de Baca of Sedillo; Tonita Sanchez and Mauricia Gonzales of Tijeras; Jesusita Jaramillo of San Antonio; Susana de Martinez of Ranchos de Albuquerque; Ignacia Chavez of Los Padillas; Refugia Avila and Manuela Arias of San Jose; Beneranda Jaramillo of Armijo; Atoche Garcia, Mariallita Jaramillo, and Moniquita Abeyta of Atrisco; and Tomasa Rivera, Juanita Martinez, Valentina Abeyta, Victoria Flores, Margarita Garcia, Alice Turpin, Eutimia Gabaldon, Luz Lopez, Refugia Mora, and Juanita Clark of Albuquerque.

When the distribution of midwives certified in 1925 Bernalillo County is mapped, Albuquerque, as opposed to more rural regions, has the highest number of midwives in one area. This indicates that, while the practice of midwifery may have occurred in greater frequency in rural New Mexico, urban areas were not exempt, and access to physicians did not mark midwives as redundant or unneeded. Based on the estimation of members of the New Mexico Medical Society in 1928 in Bernalillo County, the number of certified midwives (thirty-seven) nearly equaled the number of physicians (thirty-nine). Furthermore, this number did not include midwives that were not certified in the county who attended to births regardless of licensing requirements.

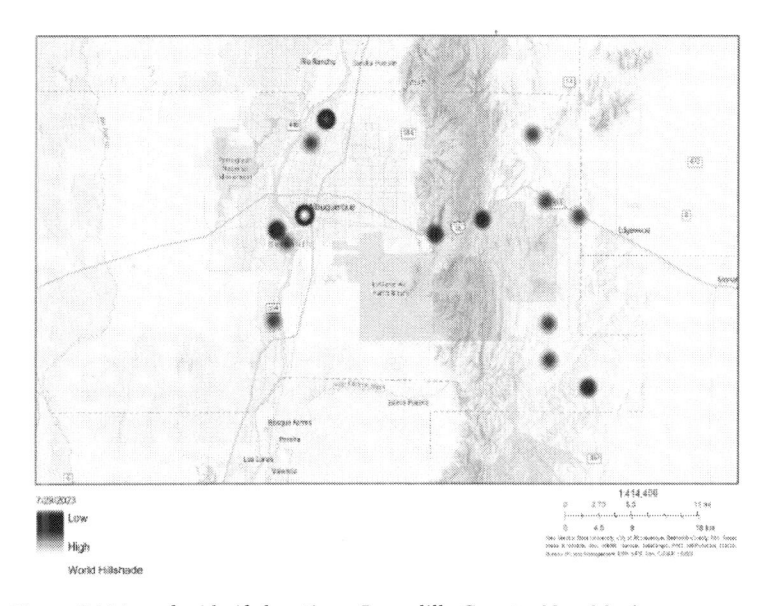

Figure 2.1 Map of midwife locations, Bernalillo County, New Mexico

Conclusion

The number of women who were certified in 1925, rather than representing the remnants of a diminishing practice of healthcare in the state, indicated a different reality that emphasized their continued necessity in New Mexico. While their numbers would eventually decline over time, the impact of their work and knowledge extended far into the twentieth century. Rather than a distinctly rural phenomenon, the work of traditional healers and midwives permeated throughout New Mexico, encouraging a system of medical pluralism, wherein patients would turn to both traditional healers and licensed physicians as resources for healthcare. This system emerged, in part, due to the continual provisions through legislation and public health initiatives to allow lay midwives to practice into the twentieth century, but it also was a result of midwife persistence to maintain their practice and patient autonomy to define their obstetric care.

References

American Medical Association. 1925. "House of Delegates Proceedings, Annual Session."

Anderson, Dorothy. 1927. "Divisions of Child Hygiene and Public Health Nursing." *Biennial Report* 5: 13–16.

Aragón, Jesusita. 1987. Living Treasures Oral History Collection, Fray Angélico Chávez History Library, Santa Fe, New Mexico.

Armus, Diego, and Pablo F. Gómez, eds. 2021. *The Gray Zones of Medicine: Healers and History in Latin America*. Pittsburgh, PA: University of Pittsburgh Press.

Atkins, Francis H. 1897. "Correspondence," *Denver Medical Times* 16 (11) May: 500.

Bureau of the Census. 1930. Alameda, Bernalillo, New Mexico. Enumeration District: 0053. Fifteenth Census of the United States, 1930. Washington, DC: National Archives and Records Administration. T626, 2,667 rolls, p. 2A, FHL microfilm 2341127.

Bureau of Public Health. 1923. Health Officers' Weekly Bulletin. June 5. New Mexico Department of Public Health Collection (HHC 28, CN 137), box 1, folder 1, Health Sciences Library and Informatics Center, University of New Mexico Libraries.

Bureau of Public Health. 1926. "Fourth Biennial Report, 1925–1926." *New Mexico Health Officer*, vol. 4, 1925-1926.

Cohenour, L.B. 1928. Report to the House of Delegates. New Mexico Medical Society Forty-Sixth Annual Meeting. May 10. p. 4. New Mexico Medical Society Records (HHC 1), University of New Mexico Health Sciences Library and Informatics Center, University of New Mexico Libraries.

Department of Public Health. 1938. "Tenth Biennial Report, 1937–1938." *New Mexico Health Officer* 7 (2).

Dunn, Halbert L. 1956. U.S. Census Bureau, National Office of Vital Statistics. 1954. Table 18. "Vital Statistics of the United States, 1954: Introduction and Summary Tables." vol. 1. Washington, DC: United States Government Printing Office.

"Editorial Correspondence." 1893. *Albuquerque Journal*, February 25.

Greenfield, Myrtle. 1962. *A History of Public Health in New Mexico*. Albuquerque, NM: University of New Mexico Press.

Holtby, David V. 2012. *Forty-Seventh Star: New Mexico's Struggle for Statehood*. Norman, OK: University of Oklahoma Press.

Kisner, J. C. 1928. "General Session." New Mexico Medical Society Forty-Sixth Annual Meeting. May 12. New Mexico Medical Society Records (HHC 1), University of New Mexico Health Sciences Library and Informatics Center, University of New Mexico Libraries.

"Legislative Chat." 1893. *Santa Fe New Mexican*, February 10.

Mckiernan-González, John. 2012. *Fevered Measures: Public Health and Race at the Texas-Mexico Border, 1848–1942*. Durham, NC: Duke University Press.

McQuade-Salzfass, Lena. 2014. "'An Indispensable Service': Midwives and Medical Officials after New Mexico Statehood." In *Precarious Prescriptions: Contested Histories of Race and Health in North America*, ed. Laurie B. Green, John McKiernan-González, and Martin Summers. Minneapolis: University of Minnesota Press, 115–41.

Meckel, Richard. 1990. *Save the Babies: American Public Health Reform and the Prevention of Infant Mortality, 1850–1929*. Baltimore, MD: Johns Hopkins University Press.

"Midwives Given Licenses After Passing Tests." 1925. *Albuquerque Morning Journal*, December 10.

Mitchell, Pablo. 2005. *Coyote Nation: Sexuality, Race, and Conquest in Modernizing New Mexico, 1880–1920*. Chicago, IL: University of Chicago Press.

New Mexico Department of Public Health. 1954. "Please, Mother, Boil the Water!" *It's Your Health Department* 9, no. 1 (October). New Mexico Department of Public Health Collection (HHC 28, CN 137), Box 2, Folder 34, Health Sciences Library and Informatics Center, University of New Mexico Libraries.

New Mexico Medical Society. 1928. "Forty-Sixth Annual Meeting." May 10–12. Unbound Annual Meetings, New Mexico Medical Society (HHC 1), Health Sciences Library and Informatics Center, University of New Mexico Libraries.

Otero, Miguel. 1899. *Report of the Governor of New Mexico to the Secretary of the Interior*. Santa Fe, NM: Government Printing Office.

Ortiz, Felina Mychelle. 2005. "History of Midwifery in New Mexico: Partnership Between Curandera-parteras and the New Mexico Department of Health." *Journal of Midwifery & Women's Health* 50 (5) September/October: 411–17.

Prince, L. Bradford. 1893. "A Scorching Veto for the Medical Bill." *The Weekly New Mexican Review*. March 2.

Sánchez, George Isidore. 1940. *Forgotten People: A Study of New Mexicans*. Albuquerque, NM: University of New Mexico Press.

Scott, James. 1944. "Twenty-Five Years of Public Health in New Mexico." *New Mexico Health Officer* 7 (3-4) December.

Spidle, Jake W., Jr. 1986. *Doctors of Medicine in New Mexico: A History of Health and Medical Practice, 1886-1986.* Albuquerque, NM: University of New Mexico Press.

Torres, Eliseo. 2006. *Healing with Herbs and Rituals: A Mexican Tradition.* Albuquerque, NM: University of New Mexico Press.

"Trained Midwives Important Feature of County Efforts for Better Babies." 1921. *Santa Fe New Mexican*, August 25.

Trennert, Robert A. 1998. *White Man's Medicine: Government Doctors and the Navajo, 1863-1955.* Albuquerque, NM: University of New Mexico Press.

van der Eerden, M. Lucia. 1948. *Maternity Care in a Spanish-American Community of New Mexico.* PhD diss., Washington, D.C.: Catholic University of America Press.

Walzer Leavitt, Judith. 1986. *Brought to Bed: Childbearing in America, 1750-1950.* New York, NY: Oxford University Press.

Whorton, Brad. 2002. *New Mexico Public Health Achievements During the 20th Century.* Santa Fe, NM: Office of New Mexico Vital Records and Health Statistics Public Health Division.

3. La Grippe's Fearful Work

Data and Narrative during the 1889–1892 Influenza in Alabama

E. THOMAS EWING

In January 1892, Dr. Frank Prince was called to the home of Sampson Thorne, an African American farmer "in good circumstances." When the physician arrived at the farm near Bessemer, Alabama, he "found two of the family dead, another dying and five seriously ill, the fearful work of the prevailing epidemic—la grippe" (Herald Journal, January 21, 1892, 2).

Three aspects of this brief newspaper article provide a useful opening to this study of the 1889–92 influenza in Alabama: the deaths of individuals, the question of race, and stories about epidemic outbreaks. This brief newspaper report provides evidence of how this disease affected individuals, as it caused two deaths, one impending death, and multiple illnesses. No further information about the victims in the family of Sampson Thorne was provided in this newspaper. The 1880 census lists Sampson (age twenty-five), his wife Nellie (age twenty), and four children, ages one to five. Twelve years later, these children would have been ages thirteen to eighteen. It is not known which two family members were dead, which one was "dying," and the fate of those who were "seriously ill." Census records from subsequent years provide results for Samson and sons Lucien, John, and Burwell, but not for wife Nellie or daughter Jane, suggesting they were the two family members who perished (US Census 1880, 1900).

This article is notable because a white newspaper commented on deaths and illness in an African American household. Jefferson County, where the Thorne family had their homestead, was 36 percent African American, according to the 1890 census. As an independent farmer, Thorne occupied a higher socioeconomic status within the African American population, which might explain why these newspapers covered this story, as well as the fact that a prominent white physician was summoned to care for this family.

Yet it is also important to recognize that the sensationalist elements of this story—two dead, one dying, and even more sick—explains the attention it received in these newspapers. The headline of the story embodied these sensational elements "La Grippe's Fearful Work: Two Dead, One Dying, and Five Seriously Ill." The final comment, that these deaths and illnesses were evidence of "the fearful work of the prevailing epidemic—la grippe," certainly reinforces this sense of sensationalism at work even as the article also expressed legitimate fears about disease and death.

Epidemics are well suited to this volume's themes of challenging stories because they involve both individual narratives and broad social impacts. In the late nineteenth century, an "epidemic" was defined as "common to many people; a prevailing disease," while a pandemic was defined as "a widespread epidemic" (Gould 1900). Current definitions from the US Centers for Disease Control and Prevention (CDC) use qualitative terms that recognize quantitative change: an "epidemic" is defined as "an increase, often sudden, in the number of cases of a disease above what is normally expected in that population in that area"; a "pandemic" is defined as "an epidemic that has spread over several countries or continents, usually affecting a large number of people" (CDC 2012). The definition of a pandemic or epidemic involves quantity, yet the modifiers are qualitative: a sudden increase, above normal expectations, usually affecting large numbers. Epidemics and pandemics are thus the cumulative experience of hundreds, thousands, and millions of individuals, who are exposed, fall ill, die, or recover from an unusually widespread outbreak of disease. During the COVID-19 pandemic, efforts to capture the impact on individuals included lists of names, displays of flags, and closely reported stories of victims, family members, and survivors. This case study is inspired by COVID Black, a project at the intersection of digital humanities, public health, and racial inequities, which fully illustrated the urgency of considering stories told by and about marginal and vulnerable populations during pandemics. COVID Black seeks to "redefine statistics and information into living data and stories about Black Health," with the goal of telling "empowering stories about Black life that address racial health disparities" (COVID Black 2020). Bringing this perspective to study a historical epidemic means asking similar questions about how data can reveal stories of marginalized or vulnerable populations and how stories about individuals and families complicate and enrich our understanding of the experience of living during, through, and beyond a pandemic.

The challenging stories revealed in this study illustrate the changes a pandemic causes in the lives of individuals, the response of medical authorities, and the experience of communities. Previous scholarship on the collection and interpretation of vital statistics, networks of information and infection, and the tension between individual outcomes and quantitative measures establishes the pathway for this case study of influenza in Alabama (Ewing 2017, 2019, 2021). This exploration of challenging stories reveals how epidemics reinforce existing structures, confirm cultural patterns, and illustrate underlying beliefs. The recent experience of COVID-19 provides tools and methods to recognize, explore, and interpret the relationship between the massive scale of a global pandemic and the individual experience of illness, death, and loss.

This chapter explores the influenza epidemic in Alabama using digitized newspapers, annual reports from the Alabama Board of Health, and vital statistics from the 1890 census (Vital Statistics 1890). These sources make it possible to understand both the scale of this epidemic and differences by region, cause of death, and race. The 1890 Census recorded Alabama's population as 1,513,017, which included 679,299 people classified as "colored" (45 percent) and 833,718 people classified as "white" (55 percent). The "colored" category included 759 people classified as "Civilized Indians," 49 as Chinese or Japanese, and 678,489 as "Negro descent." The last of these categories included 601,069 Negroes, 65,993 Mulattoes, 7,040 Quadroons, and 4,387 Octoroons. The 1890 census was the only decennial census to use four different categories to classify African Americans. Alabama was one of six states, all in the Southeast, where the African American population made up 40 percent or more of the total population. Alabama accounted for 9 percent of the total African American population in the United States but just 1 percent of the total white population, further illustrating the concentration of African American populations in the southeastern United States.

Deaths during the Epidemic

The introductory sections for each annual report from the Alabama Board of Health offer an official narrative of the quantitative impact of this pandemic. The 1890 report indicated that Alabama had "no serious epidemic visitation, at least none that required any direct intervention of the State Board of Health." All regions of the state "suffered from the grippe, or epidemic influenza, which, by reason of various complications, has added some small percentage to the usual death rates" (Alabama Health Report 1890). The 1891 Annual Report described how the state had been "visited by only one great epidemic invasion—influenza or grippe." The disease began in northern Alabama and gradually spread in a southern direction: "Very few sections of the State escaped it, and its prevalence was widespread and general." The disease was generally mild, particularly in the southern regions that were affected later, but mortality rates increased, usually due to complications associated with pneumonia (Alabama Health Report 1891). The 1892 report, by contrast, declared that "no destructive epidemic has invaded our state," as the population has been "free from yellow fever, cholera, and smallpox." The report recognized "local and sporadic outbreaks" of grippe along with scarlet fever and diphtheria but declared that "none of these have added greatly to the mortality" (Alabama Health Report 1892). This statement is surprising given that total deaths from la grippe in 1892 were higher than in either preceding year.

A review of Alabama newspapers in early 1890 illustrates how the narrative of the epidemic shifted from distant to local reporting as the disease progressed from Europe to the northeastern United States and then into southern states such as Alabama (Ewing 2023). The first mention of the unusual disease outbreak in an Alabama newspaper appeared in early December with a brief report on the "epidemic of influenza" in St. Petersburg, Russia (*Huntsville Gazette*, December 7, 1889, 1). In the weeks that followed, newspapers reported on the disease across Europe and then in New York City. These reports consistently communicated the message that influenza, while causing many people to become sick, was "not considered very dangerous" (*Cullman Tribune*, December 19, 1889, 3).

Early in 1890, Alabama newspapers began to report on local cases. On January 2, 1890, the *Times and News* reported that the "entire post office" in the small town of Eufaula "is grappling with 'la grippe' or Russian influenza," as postal officials warned of "consequences" if "something is not done soon to relieve them" (*Times and News*, January 2, 1890, 3). On the same day, the *Times-Democrat* in Wetumpka included this statement: "George Smith says he caught the La Grippe known as influenza" (*Times-Democrat*, January 2, 1890, 5). These very brief reports are illustrative of this first stage of the epidemic, as they indicate awareness of the pandemic in other locations, as suggested by terms such as "Russian influenza," yet they count relatively few cases at the local level. The report on the Eufaula post office confirms the potential threat of this outbreak by indicating how widespread illness leading to absenteeism at work could produce noticeable consequences for the public.

Alabama newspapers consistently predicted that the outbreak would have only mild consequences. On January 9, 1890, for example, the *Bibb Blade*, published in Six Mile, stated that influenza "is not considered by the doctors to be fatal except when complicated by other diseases" (*Bibb Blade*, January 9, 1890, 2). On the same day, a "prominent physician" in Birmingham declared that he was treating "about a dozen cases" but all were mild "and none likely to prove serious" (*Birmingham News*, January 9, 1890, 6). Dr. Jay in Evergreen, Alabama, offered a similarly optimistic prognosis: "I do not think that the type of it we have here is anything more than a very bad cold, attended with an aggravated sore throat. I do not believe, with proper care, it will ever prove fatal" (*Montgomery Advertiser*, January 10, 1890, 2).

By the second week of January 1890, however, Alabama newspapers were reporting on more widespread cases of influenza. In Birmingham, "several hundred cases of influenza" were reported, with outbreaks especially widespread around train stations where personnel "came in contact with the traveling public." According to a prominent local physician, most downtown businesses had two or three cases, yet "a remarkable fact" is that "not a single serious case or death from the disease has been reported." Even this report of widespread cases ended with a humorous observation that city leaders "have laid in an extra supply of handkerchiefs" and are "ready for a siege of the pest" (*Birmingham News*, January 11, 1890, 6).

The first death from influenza located in Alabama newspapers was reported in late January, about three weeks after the first cases. Albert L. Smart, aged thirty-eight, died on January 25, in Clio, where he lived with his wife and children. Smart complained of "feeling unwell" and expressed concern that "he had taken the prevailing epidemic influenza." The disease "developed into pneumonia and carried him off," according to the obituary (*Times and News*, January 30, 1890, 3). More death reports followed in subsequent weeks and months, yet obituaries specifically attributing deaths to influenza or related diseases appeared only rarely in Alabama newspapers. On January 31, Henry Carter, "a well known and highly thought of colored [sic] citizen," died "rather suddenly" from "an attack of La Grippe" (*Marion Times-Standard*, February 5, 1890, 5). On February 12, Mary Stone Armstrong died "suddenly" after suffering for several days of "cold or influenza," until her condition worsened and led to her death (*Weekly Advertiser*, February 13, 1890, 2). On March 18, Dr. Egbert Johnson, the thirty-two-year-old city physician in Eufaula, died of "pneumonia, preceded by la grippe" (*Eufaula Daily Times*, March 19, 1890, 4).

The frequency of deaths from influenza reported in Alabama newspapers appeared to decrease over the rest of 1890, but then increased again at the start of the new year, marking both the seasonality of influenza and the return of an epidemic wave. On January 8, 1891, the *Weekly Advertiser* declared that the "dreadful but fashionable disease, La Grippe, is again raging throughout the country" and is "having a day in Montgomery," with physicians reporting "several hundred cases in the city, with the list increasing daily." Yet the "disease appears here in a very mild form, and there have been no fatalities so far." The newspaper reassured the public "it is not likely that the disease will make any serious headway in Montgomery" (*Weekly Advertiser*, January 8, 1891, 2). Reports of increasing disease appeared more frequently across the state in subsequent days; they mentioned "many cases of grippe" in Birmingham (*Birmingham News*, January 13, 1891, 7), a "large number of our citizens are suffering with the la grippe" in Brewton (*Standard Gauge*, January 15, 1891, 3), and "grippe is still raging" in Sheffield (*Sheffield Weekly Enterprise*, January 16, 1891, 1).

Newspapers began to report more deaths from this disease or associated causes in late January and early February 1891, the second wave of the pandemic. Major Halliday, "one of Auburn's oldest and most estimable citizens," died on January 9, 1891: "he was taken with the grippe last week, which developed into pneumonia, and the latter disease soon conquered the old gentleman's frail body" (*Montgomery Advertiser*, January 10, 1891, 2). On January 11, Jesse L. Adams, "one of the eldest and extensively known citizens of Tuskegee," died of "grippe, which later developed into pneumonia" (*Weekly Advertiser*, January 15, 1891, 6). One of the rare examples of a child victim of this disease was reported in Greenville, where "little Annie," daughter of Mr. and Mrs. C. F. McCarthy, died "of la grippe" on January 18, 1891 (*Greenville Advocate*, January 21, 1891, 3). A few days later, the deaths of two Fort Deposit residents, Gena Stewart Roper and Dr. R. P. Means, were cited as evidence that "this disease is proving quite fatal in many localities" (*Montgomery Advertiser*, January 21, 1891, 4). In Montgomery, John C. Woolfolk was "first taken with la grippe, which went into pneumonia," causing a death that left a widow and four children (*Montgomery Advertiser*, January 23, 1891, 5). W. P. Thompson, the mayor of Tuskegee, died "after a sickness of only three or four days with la grippe," at a time when "half the people of that town are reported sick with la grippe" (*Tuskegee News*, January 24, 1891, 1). Billie Martin, a "well-known and highly respected" resident of Luverne, "was first attacked with la grippe, which resulted in pneumonia, causing his death" (*Troy Messenger*, January 29, 1891, 5). At the end of January 1891, Frank Boykin, age forty, died near Union Springs after a sudden "attack of la grippe" led to "congestion of the lungs" (*Montgomery Advertiser*, January 30, 1891, 8).

A third wave of the pandemic in late 1891 and early 1892 prompted further reports of deaths caused by influenza and related conditions. In Montgomery, the Rev. Dr. William Harris died of "la grippe, which had laid him up since last week, culminating in congestion of the lungs" (*Eufaula Daily Times*, December 29, 1891, 2). In Huntsville, Britton Franks, age eighty-four, died in late December 1891 "of grippe after a few days illness" (*Guntersville Democrat*, January 7, 1892, 3). Lawrence Fisher, a clerk in a Birmingham railway freight office, died at age thirty-nine after three weeks of illness "with the grippe" (*Birmingham News*, January 5, 1892, 3). Laura Somerville fell seriously ill with "the trouble grippe," which "developed rapidly into pneumonia," leading to death (*Tuscaloosa Weekly Times*, January 6, 1892, 3). The *Alabama Inquirer*, published in Hartselle, reported three deaths from "la grippe" in the January 13 issue: Mr. Wm. Lindsey, Mrs. D. C. Puckett, and Mrs. Wm. Fricke (*Alabama Inquirer*, January 13, 1892). In late January, W. H. Rogers, age fifty, died of la grippe, leaving a widow and five children. (*Alabama Inquirer*, January 28, 1892, 3). In early February 1892, Associate Justice David Clopton of the Alabama Supreme Court died as "an attack of La Grippe" developed into pneumonia, which became "the immediate cause of death" (*Alabama Beacon*, February

9, 1892, 3). In Gadsden, John T. Martin, age forty-seven, had been "critically ill" for almost six weeks before his death in early February (*Montgomery Advertiser*, February 10, 1892, 2). In a county west of Pratville, A. G. Caver, age seventy-three, died "with the grippe" (*Prattville Progress*, February 19, 1892, 4).

In addition to reporting individual deaths, this third phase of the pandemic prompted some newspapers to comment on the scope of the disease. In late December 1891, a report in the *Birmingham News* described the Livingstone family where a son, his mother, and a sister all died within a few days, all from "the now prevalent malady, the grippe" (*Birmingham News*, December 30, 1891, 4). In early February 1892, R. J. Stephenson, who lived near Moulton, declared that "La Grippe has taken people at a fearful rate," with four deaths and two quite ill in one family (*Moulton Advertiser*, February 4, 1892, 3). In LaFayette, a report on February 19, 1892, stated that four citizens had died "from la grippe" in the past ten days, and more than fifty cases were reported: "Nothing like it has ever been known before in that place" (*Birmingham News*, February 19, 1892, 3). These reports, like the report on deaths in the Thorne family which opened this chapter, demonstrate how "La Grippe's Fearful Work" occurred throughout the years of this pandemic.

Statistics during the Epidemic

These impressions of a widespread and severe outbreak of disease in newspaper editorials and commentaries can be compared to the statistics reported by the state board of health and the US Census. The Vital Statistics published by the Alabama Board of Health provide quantitative evidence of the impact of this influenza epidemic. The annual report on vital statistics included 625 deaths attributed to la grippe during the pandemic years: seventy-five deaths in 1890, 247 in 1891, and 303 in 1892 (Alabama Health Report, 1890, 1891, 1892). By contrast, just five deaths were attributed to this cause in the three years preceding the pandemic: four deaths in 1887 (attributed to influenza), zero deaths in 1888, and one death in 1889. A chart based on monthly statistics illustrates the notable increase in deaths in January, February, and March 1890, a greater increase of deaths in the same months in 1891, and the most dramatic increase in the first quarter of 1892. In fact, one-half of all deaths from la grippe during this three-year period took place in just three months from January to March 1892.

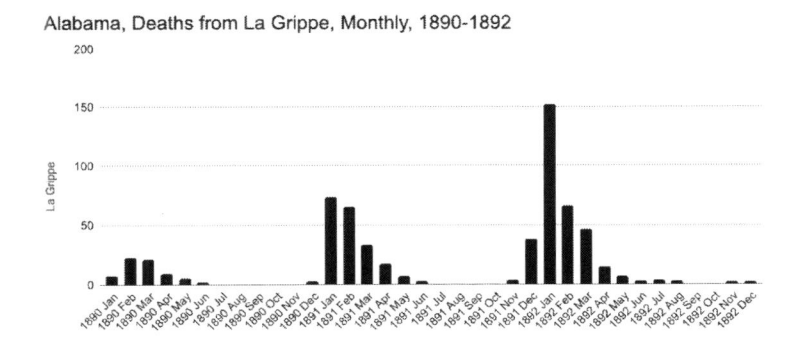

Alabama, Deaths from La Grippe, Monthly, 1890-1892

Figure 3.1

These reports confirm the trajectory of the epidemic noted in newspapers, including the fact that the greatest number of deaths attributed to this one disease occurred in the third year of the pandemic, from December 1891 to March 1892.

Yet this analysis of influenza statistics must begin with recognition that state reports were incomplete. This discrepancy is clearly illustrated by the fact that the US Census reported just over 20,000 deaths in Alabama in the twelve months of the census year, from June 1889 to May 1890 (US Census 1890), yet the annual reports for 1889 and 1890 reported approximately 10,000 deaths each year. In other words, the US Census reported almost twice as many deaths as the state health board for the same length of time. Less than half of the sixty-six counties in Alabama have consistent reports on deaths in the annual reports for 1890, 1891, and 1892. The twenty-six counties that provided consistent data allowing for meaningful comparisons accounted for one-half of the total population; the percent of African Americans in this sample was slightly higher than the percent in the state population. Some reporting counties had a majority Black population of 75 percent or more (Lowndes, Dallas, Hale, Bullock, and Montgomery Counties), while other reporting counties had a majority white population of 75 percent or more (Morgan, St. Clair, Jackson, Clay, and Dekalb Counties). The annual reports are thus helpful for identifying trends in timing, cause of death, and racial distribution, but they are incomplete and thus cannot be used as sources for total numbers for the state during these years. The US Census did not begin annual reports on vital statistics until the early 1900s, so the state records, while incomplete, remain the best source for exploring data about this pandemic.

The total number of deaths from all cases in Alabama reported by the state board of health decreased in each successive year: 9,722 deaths in 1890, 8,110 deaths in 1891, and 7,823 deaths in 1892. The death rate for both races also decreased during these three years.

Table 3.1: Death Rates by Year (per thousand)

Death rate	1890	1891	1892
African American	7.4	6.3	6.0
White	5.7	4.6	4.5

These statistics reveal an anomalous pattern, however, which is suggestive of both infection patterns and the social meanings of disease, as indicated in table 3.2, which compares deaths from influenza and pneumonia by race during each year of the pandemic.

Table 3.2: La Grippe and Pneumonia Deaths by Cause, Race, and Year

	Deaths (Total)	White (Total)	White (Rate / 100,000)	African American (Total)	African American (Rate / 100,000)
1890					
All causes	9,722	4,716	565.7	5,006	737.8
La Grippe	**75**	**48**	**5.8**	**27**	**4.0**
Pneumonia	772	365	43.8	407	60.0
1891					
All causes	8,110	3,840	460.6	4,270	629.3
La Grippe	**247**	**127**	**15.2**	**120**	**17.7**
Pneumonia	699	313	37.5	386	56.9
1892					
All causes	7,823	3,721	446.3	4,102	604.6
La Grippe	**303**	**179**	**21.5**	**124**	**18.3**
Pneumonia	697	323	38.7	374	56.9

Whereas death rates from all causes and from pneumonia were consistently higher for the African American population, the death rates from la grippe were more similar across the racial boundaries in 1890 and 1891 and were actually higher for the white population in 1892, when the most deaths from la grippe were recorded in the state.

The limitations in vital statistics can be partially addressed by examining interpretations about the number of deaths among white and African American populations. White newspapers in Alabama rarely reported on deaths among African American populations related to the pandemic; the obituary for Henry Carter in the *Marion Times-Standard* cited previously was exceptional in this context. The few examples of white newspapers reporting on deaths among African Americans are notable for what they say—and what was omitted or distorted. On February 27, 1890, the *Shelby News* published a report: "La Grippe seems to be very fatal among the negroes of this neighborhood. Three or four deaths in the last week" (*Shelby News*, February 27, 1890, 4). In Shelby County, African Americans were just under one-third of the total population, but no monthly data for Shelby County was published in the 1890 annual report.

Two weeks later, the *Choctaw Herald*, published in Butler, reported that "La Grippe, in some localities of this section is raging among the negroes. We hear of several deaths during the past few days." In the days that followed, a similar, but briefer, report appeared elsewhere in the state: "Negroes are dying of La Grippe in Choctaw County" (statement published in *Montgomery Advertiser*, March 18, 1890, 8; *Sumter County Sun*, March 20, 1890, 2; *Alabama Inquirer*, March 27, 1890, 1). According to the 1890 census, the African American population in Choctaw County made up a slight majority. In March 1890, according to the state health board report, Choctaw County recorded a total of thirteen deaths, including six whites and four African Americans (the race of the other three deaths was not specified). If the newspaper reports were correct, the "several deaths" from la grippe in early March would seemingly account for all the deaths recorded by the state health board for the entire month.

In the *Livingston Journal*, a note from the small town of McGainville, signed with the name REX, declared that "nearly every family around here has been attacked" and some "have suffered considerably." The correspondent offered this personal observation and commentary: "So far, none of the whites have died with it, but I have heard of several [B]lacks dying. I suppose the cause of its being more fatal with the [B]lacks is on account of their not taking proper care of themselves" (*Livingston Journal*, January 29, 1892, 5). In Hale County, where African Americans made up more than three-quarters of the population, the eleven deaths in 1892 were more than double the total of five white deaths, yet the rate for African Americans was lower than for whites. Over the three years of the pandemic, the death rate for whites and African Americans in Hale County was exactly the same: 8.2 deaths per 1,000 population. The white rate was higher in 1890 and 1891 yet lower in 1892, when the most deaths from influenza were recorded by the state board of health.

The 1891 Annual Report commented on the "remarkable fact" that the grippe "attacked" African Americans "to a much less extent than the white population" and African Americans "seem to have been comparatively exempt from it" (Alabama Health Report 1891). Yet these reports are suggestive of broader discourse that identified African American health as a social problem using a racist framework that attributed higher mortality to physiological and social traits of this marginalized population (Torchia 1975; Byrd and Clayton 1992; Gamble 1997; Roberts 2009). Understanding reporting on African Americans during the Russian influenza requires an appreciation of the complicated discourse on disease, medicine, and health in the US South in the decades following the Civil War.

Conclusion

The COVID-19 pandemic has demonstrated the importance of understanding how the experience of living with the threat of deadly diseases shapes perceptions, interactions, and expectations (Nurridin, Mooney, White 2020). During the Russian flu pandemic, newspaper articles provide similar insights into perceptions, interactions, and expectations by relating the stories of individual victims in the form of obituaries and death notices. Statistical reports from the US Census and the Alabama Board of Health provide quantitative evidence of the impact of this pandemic on the state population with some additional insights into the timing of deaths and the differential impact by race. During the Russian flu, as would be the case again during the COVID-19 pandemic, counting became a site of contested meaning, as regulatory agencies used numerical representations to impose policies and practices on populations even as the evidence that this data was incomplete, inconsistent, or inaccurate became weapons used by those seeking to resist, obstruct, or repudiate health policies intended to protect the well-being of the whole society.

In late nineteenth century America, death rates were consistently higher in southeastern states among the African American population, due to structural racism in access to healthcare, housing, work, infant mortality, childhood diseases, and other conditions. In Alabama, according to the 1890 census, the death rate from all causes was 12.3 deaths per 1,000 for the white population and 15.6 deaths per 1,000 for the "Colored" population. The fact that the "Colored" rate was nearly 20 percent higher confirms the greater vulnerability to all causes of death, and particularly infectious disease, among the members of this minoritized population. The death rate from specific causes, however, indicated greater disparities, which further illustrated the importance of contextual factors: the death rate for consumption (tuberculosis) for the "Colored" population was twice the rate for the white population, while the death rate from pneumonia was only 50 percent higher. Given that the influenza epidemic exacerbated respiratory diseases, it seems likely that the discrepancy in death rates would have increased during the epidemic.

Yet the racial line is surprisingly challenging to locate in either the stories of victims or statistical reports on the epidemic. The only Black newspaper available for this era, the *Huntsville Times*, published very few obituaries about African American victims of the epidemic. White newspapers, by contrast, regularly published obituaries identifying influenza as a cause of death, yet these newspapers rarely reported on African American victims. The board of health annual reports provided granular data about race, cause of death, county, and month in the annual reports, but these reports are obviously incomplete, as the state annual report only includes numbers from counties that submitted reports on deaths.

This case study confirms the importance of thinking critically about the spaces between data and narrative. Statistical tables contain information, but they also contain gaps. In some cases, these gaps are made visible: in the case of the Alabama health reports, counties that did not provide reports on deaths by month have empty lines in the tables. In other cases, the gaps are not visible. In the health board reports, for example, race was listed in binary terms ("white" or "colored"), yet the census data indicates people in multiple categories, including those listed as "mulatto" who occupied a liminal (but not legal) space between categories. Many statistical tables do not list influenza as a separate cause of death, which is a striking omission during a pandemic.

The Alabama Board of Health annual reports thus contain spaces that can be partially filled with stories of individual victims, as reported in newspapers. These stories situate the pandemic period in the broader narrative of a life, as some of the more detailed obituaries offered biographical information that included education, family, employment, and service. Yet other obituaries provided only a sentence or two about the time and cause of deaths. Obituaries are thus a particular form of challenging stories, yet these records are incomplete as well. These obituaries were located using key words such as "grippe" or "influenza," so victims of these diseases whose obituaries did not list this cause of death will likely be absent from this study. Obituaries also have notable silences related to age, gender, class, and race: infants rarely received public notice of deaths and men were more likely to appear in newspapers (although some women's deaths were noted), as were prominent individuals based on family background. Employment and social status were more likely to be described in more detail, and, as discussed above, white newspapers rarely reported on deaths of African Americans, even in counties where white people were in the minority.

The story about the Thorne family that began this chapter thus needs to be understood in the context of a pandemic disease outbreak. During a three-year period, one disease, la grippe, claimed an unusually high number of lives, even as death totals and rates remained stable or even declined. In contrast to the 1918 influenza epidemic or COVID-19 in 2020, this pandemic did not appear to result in an overall increase in death rates in Alabama. Each individual case or death was a story about the challenges of living in the context of a pandemic, where disease mattered in daily lives, in newspapers, and in statistical collections.

References

Alabama Beacon (Greensboro, Alabama)
Alabama Inquirer (Anniston, Alabama)
Bibb Blade (Six Mile, Alabama)
Birmingham News (Birmingham, Alabama)
Choctaw Herald (Butler, Alabama)
Cullman Tribune (Cullman, Alabama)
Eufaula Daily Times (Eufala, Alabama)
Greenville Advocate (Greenville, Alabama)
Guntersville Democrat (Guntersville, Alabama)

Herald Journal (Bessemer, Alabama)
Huntsville Gazette (Huntsville, Alabama)
Huntsville Times (Huntsville, Alabama)
Livingston Journal (Livingston, Alabama)
Marion Times-Standard (Marion, Alabama)
Montgomery Advertiser (Montgomery, Alabama)
Moulton Advertiser (Moulton, Alabama)
Prattville Progress (Prattville, Alabama)
Sheffield Weekly Enterprise (Sheffield, Alabama)
Shelby News (Calera, Alabama)
Standard Gauge (Brewton, Alabama)
Sumter County Sun (Livingston, Alabama)
Times and News (Eufaula, Alabama)
Times-Democrat (Wetumpka, Alabama)
Troy Messenger (Troy, Alabama)
Tuscaloosa Weekly Times (Tuscaloosa, Alabama)
Tuskegee News (Tuskegee, Alabama)
Weekly Advertiser (Montgomery, Alabama)

Alabama Health Report. 1890. *Board of Health of the State of Alabama Report for the Year 1890*. Montgomery, AL: Brown Printing Co.

Alabama Health Report. 1891. *Board of Health of the State of Alabama Report for the Year 1891*. Montgomery, AL: Brown Printing Co.

Alabama Health Report. 1892. *Board of Health of the State of Alabama Report for the Year 1892*. Montgomery, AL: Brown Printing Co.

Byrd, W. Michael, and Linda A. Clayton. 1992. "An American Health Dilemma: A History of Blacks in the Health System." *Journal of the National Medical Association* 84 (2): 189–200.

Centers for Disease Control and Prevention (CDC). 2012. *Principles of Epidemiology*. Atlanta, GA: US Department of Health and Human Services, Public Health Service, Centers for Disease Control.

COVID Black. 2020. Kim Gallon, founder. Black Health Heritage Data Lab, Brown University. Digital Humanities Website.

Ewing, E. Thomas. 2017. "'Will It Come Here?' Using Digital Humanities Tools to Explore Medical Understanding during the Russian Flu Epidemic, 1889–90." *Medical History* 61 (3) July: 474–77.

Ewing, E. Thomas. 2019. "La Grippe or Russian Influenza: Mortality Statistics during the 1890 Epidemic in Indiana." *Influenza and Other Respiratory Viruses* 13 (13) May: 279–87.

Ewing, E. Thomas. 2021. "'The Most Disastrous and Fatal Epidemic': Mortality Statistics During the 1890 Russian Influenza Epidemic in Connecticut." *Public Health Reports* 137 (1) March: 17–24.

Ewing, E. Thomas. 2023. "'Have We La Grippe?': A Washington Case Study of Reporting the 'Russian Influenza' (1889–1890)." In *Journalists and Knowledge Practices: Histories of Observing the Everyday in the Newspaper Age*, ed. Hansjakob Ziemer, 50-69. New York, NY: Routledge.

Gamble, Vanessa Northington. 1997. "Under the Shadow of Tuskegee: African Americans and Health Care." *American Journal of Public Health* 87: 1773–78.

Gould, George M. 1900. *A Pocket Medical Dictionary*. Philadelphia, PA: P. Blakiston's Son.

Nuriddin, Ayah, Graham Mooney, and Alexandre I. R. White. 2020. "Reckoning with Histories of Medical Racism and Violence in the USA." *Lancet* 396 (October): 949–51.

Roberts, Samuel Kelton, Jr. 2009. *Infectious Fear: Politics, Disease, and the Health Effects of Segregation*. Chapel Hill, NC: University of North Carolina Press.

Torchia, Maron M. 1975. "The Tuberculosis Movement and the Race Question, 1890–1950." *Bulletin of the History of Medicine* 49 (2) Summer: 152–68.

US Census (1880, 1900). Individual census records for Thorne family, available from ancestry library edition.

Vital Statistics. 1890. *US Census, Report on Vital and Social Statistics of the United States at the Eleventh Census; Part III: Statistics of Deaths*. Washington, DC: Government Printing Office, 1894.

4. Rethinking Techniques of Bleeding in Twentieth Century Iran

SAMIN RASHIDBEIGI

Razi Public Hospital is located in the southwest of the capital Tehran. On a fall morning in 1954, a young man, Ali, checked in at the hospital. It was shortly after 8 a.m. when he was guided to the hospital's lab. Ali was there to donate blood. He explained to the lab's supervisor that he had made a vow to self-flagellate every year on the day of Ashura, in commemoration of the martyrdom of the third Shi'i Imam, Hossein.[1] But this year, he decided that instead of self-flagellation, he would donate some of his blood to the anemic patients (Puya 1954, 1, 5).

That early morning encounter captivated the lab supervisor, Dr. Puya. A few days later, Puya wrote a passionate piece in the newspaper praising Ali's good deed. In his essay, he envisioned a unique opportunity: "This incident proves that among Iranians there are plenty of such young men who, when properly guided, would make any kind of sacrifice." Puya expanded upon Ali's initiative to suggest a broader course of action: "Now that some young men in our country vowed to shed blood every year in the

---

1. Ashura is the tenth day of Muharram, the first month in the Islamic calendar. For Shi'i Muslims, it marks the day that Husayn ibn Ali, the grandson of the Islamic prophet Muhammad, was martyred in the Battle of Karbala (October 10, 680 AD). Mourning for the incident began almost immediately after the battle. Among Shi'i Muslims, Ashura is a major holy day and occasion for ritual mourning. As for self-flagellation, which is an act of commemoration, the Shi'i communities in Iraq, Lebanon, India, and Iran have performed the practice on the Day of Ashura. In the Iranian context, the earliest reference to self-flagellation as an act of mourning dates back to the late Safavid period (Calmard 1996; Chelkowski 1985; Ende 1978; Pinault 1992).

path of Imam Hussain . . . , it would be great if ulama, experts, and physicians prescribed that the blood of these people be collected for the sake of the desperate and anemic patients" (Puya 1954, 1, 5). Although Tehran had developed a basic infrastructure of blood transfusion by 1954, blood was scarce at medical institutions. Altruistic blood donations were still rare, and those who donated blood sold it in exchange for money (Ameri 2000; Azizi, Hossein, Nayernouri, and Bahadori 2015). Puya's excitement about his encounter with Ali, and his consequent newspaper proposal, were stimulated by the reality of blood shortage. To Puya, a pioneer hematologist and one of the most visible proponents of transfusion, encouraging the self-flagellators to donate blood, instead of "wasting" it, promised a solution.

This essay explores the ways that Puya and Ali made sense of this blood transaction. While the substance of exchange, meaning blood, in this scene is singular and bounded, I understand the intentions around it as multitudinous and even in tension. The blood that Ali left at the Razi Hospital is implicated in an entirely different history than that which Puya received for transfusion purposes. The story that Puya tells to the readers, even if Ali was an imaginary character, offers a unique opportunity for thinking about the multiplicity in the meaning of transfusable blood and thus draws attention to the prehistories of blood transfusion.

Exploring primary sources produced by ordinary Iranians, officials, European physicians, and international travelers, this chapter studies practices involving the extraction of blood from the body with the help of external tools, thus resembling, to a certain extent, the extraction of blood for transfusions in the twentieth century. Through examining techniques of traditional bloodletting and religious self-flagellation, this chapter argues that Iranians did not conceptualize blood transfusion merely as a techno-medical achievement. Instead, Iranians associated these practices with earlier histories of and anxieties about human blood. While focusing on the larger social, ideological, and technological forces that shaped the conceptualization of blood, this chapter makes visible and traces the changing relationships that individuals experienced with their blood over the course of the twentieth century as a way to explore challenging stories at the intersection of individual behavior, cultural contexts, and political narratives.

During the early twentieth century in Iran, blood outside of the body was primarily conceptualized as an excess and as a form of pollution. The rise of modern biomedical sciences and public health gradually yet steadily transformed bleeding into a symbol of backwardness. In the middle of the twentieth century, at the time of Ali's donation cited above, bleeding was discouraged, as blood now was perceived as an epistemic indicator and a form of medicine with revelatory and life-saving powers. This case study reminds us how the body and its fluids are contextual and contingent and thus historical subjects relate to their body and their bodily substances in myriad ways. This chapter thus emphasizes that considering "the body proper" as a "biological given," and an object of study and care exclusively in the medical context, limits our understanding of human corporeal experiences (Lock and Farquhar 2007).

The two practices of drawing blood reviewed in this chapter, one religious and one medical, were widely practiced before the advent of blood transfusion in Iran. Understanding this "before" is necessary, at least in the Iranian context, because as it was noted earlier, up to the late 1970s, the civic population displayed little interest in donating blood for noncommercial reasons. This disinterest led to a semiformal market that sustained the medical facilities with blood products primarily collected from the urban poor, often tainted or low in red blood cells as the result of immoderate donations. This chapter thus locates this disinterest in medical transfusion by asking how similar practices involving the extraction of blood from the human body generated systemic anxieties in the decades that followed at a time of escalating social and political tensions in modern Iranian history.

Matter out of Place

Before the modern biomedical sciences began to appropriate blood as a medium in the form of blood tests or as a medicine, as whole blood or blood fractions, blood and its extraction had long served its owners in various cultural and remedial contexts in Iran. In the twentieth century, medical bloodletting was by far one of the most popular therapeutics among medical practitioners and ordinary Iranians. In the case of both self-flagellation and bloodletting, however, it was not the substance of blood itself that fulfilled a specific purpose. Instead, it was its extraction, its dumping, its leaving of a mark outside of the body, and its perceived reduction inside the body that accomplished the main objective. This section asks how self-flagellators and bleeders made sense of their lost blood. Did they care much about it? Did they feel that their sense of bodily integrity was jeopardized by discharging blood? Or did they simply consider this blood a form of waste or, to use Mary Douglas's term, "matter out of place?" (Douglas 1976).

The available historical accounts indicate that self-flagellation in Iran has generally followed a standardized sequence (Calmard 1996; Chelkowski 1985; Ende 1978; Pinault 1992). Every year, on the tenth of Muharram, a group of mourners, usually young men, wearing loose white outfits that symbolized a shroud, participated in the public lamentation of the third Shi'i Imam, Hossein, and his followers, who, according to the narrative, were tragically killed at the Battle of Karbala. The commemorations were led by a storyteller (*rowzeh-khān*), who mournfully and loudly recited the tragic events of Ashura (Aghaie 2004). Throughout the ceremony, self-flagellating volunteers struck their often-shaved forehead with a small dagger (*qameh*) and thus bled. First-hand accounts of self-flagellation have often associated the ritual with hysteria and stimulation. The self-flagellator might lose his control and overdo the hitting, and another participant may have to intervene and stop him (Shahribaf 2005; Safari 1992). Some self-flagellators faint due to losing massive amounts of blood, and therefore, their fellow participants have to move them away from the others participating in the ceremony (Kasravi 2005). Nonetheless, some self-flagellators created a reputation for themselves because of their bold performances. A man in the city of Ardabil, for example, was recognized among the locals for his extreme engagement in the practice; accordingly "one could hear the crashing sound of qameh hitting the skull" (Safari 1992). Such accounts suggest how self-flagellation, as an observable action, created forms of social recognition in the community, and therefore, could potentially impact one's relationship with others.

The visual aspect of self-flagellation gained the most attention; one willfully bleeds and exposes his bleeding body to the public. The ritual was never practiced in private; it always required an audience. Participants would never wipe off their blood after hitting themselves with the *qameh*, instead allowing blood to run over their forehead and face, staining their white garment. The obligatory white color of a self-flagellator's outfit created a visual exception to the rest of the crowd costumed in black. The color white would reinforce the visibility of the blood stains. Extracted and exposed blood expressed complex meanings. Blood represented the loyalty of the practitioner to the suffering of the third Imam: "If [they] could not bleed with [Imam Hossein] and his followers, [they] would do it in the here and now." But the performance also manifested the courage and high tolerance of the self-flagellator to suffer and bleed. That's why for the "coward vow-takers" afraid to perform the practice themselves but committed to their vow, the barber and his razor would do the job on their foreheads (Shahribaf 2005, 409–11). The visibility and publicity of the performance were indispensable to the practice. It is important to note that the state's bans of self-flagellation in Iran targeted only the public aspect of the practice, meaning that individuals could and continued to perform the practice in private.

Figure 4.1: A group of men in Tabas after self-flagellation (Hedin 1910)

If not severely injured, immediately after the ceremony, the self-flagellator was expected to cleanse off the blood from his body (Shahribaf 2005, 409). In the Islamic system of ritual purity (*ṭahāra*), the act of shedding blood corrupted one's state of purity and thus the blood spilled by self-flagellation was essentially considered unclean (*najes*). Despite its temporarily glamorous life in the ceremony of Ashura, this blood was capable of polluting any surface it touched, and thus residual blood had to be immediately neutralized (Katz 2002). The temporality of this blood determined its function and its fate. On the day of Ashura, the act of bleeding and the very matter of blood, exhibited and emphasized, marked the believer's devotion to a religious narrative. Nonetheless, after the ceremony, this blood was conceptualized as a form of pollution, lifeless, useless, and out of place. Therefore, it had to be ritually cleansed and made to physically disappear from sight.

After the rise of Reza Shah to power in 1925, Pahlavi authorities banned the public commemorations of Ashura, which also included self-flagellation. The ban was part of a larger reformist project, as the new regime regarded such performances as superstition (Afary 2015). Accordingly, police and other authorities were ordered to review and prevent incidents of self-flagellation ("Gozāresh-e Jelow-giri" 1930; "Nafy-ye Qameh-zani" 1933). On some occasions, the police negotiated with the elders to advise their communities against it ("Nafy-ye Qameh-zani" 1933). But even before the state-sponsored prohibition of self-flagellation, some Shi'i *mujtahids* (legal experts) had issued *fatwas* (nonbearing legal rulings) against the practice and forbade it (*Dast-e penhān* 2008). The religious authorities barred the practice using two principal justifications. First, they argued that self-flagellation was a form of self-harming (*ezrār beh nafs*), which was condemned in the Sharia. Second, they warned that the bold spectacle of self-flagellation would lead to the association of Islam with ignorance and thus misrepresent it (*vahn-e din*) (*Dast-e penhān* 2008). Despite these prohibitions by secular and religious authorities, some Iranians, in public and private where the audience was smaller, continued to perform self-flagellation devotedly. Fischer's observation in his ethnography during the 1980s is remarkable: "A few years ago the police wanted to stop the slashing of the foreheads in a village near Tehran. Their successful strategy was to keep women away from the route of the male march" (Fischer 2003). It was within this context that Dr. Puya took interest in the possibility of marrying blood donation with the intention of self-flagellation.

During this same period, self-flagellation was not the only practice that put Iranians in touch with their blood. Bloodletting in various forms illustrated a much larger, more prevalent network of practices, meanings, actors, and regulations. Adopting Galenico-Avicennian medicine, Iranians for centuries had believed that blood was made in the liver and flowed into the heart, where it supposedly gained vital spirits. Galenico-Avicennian medicine refers to a synthesis of medical knowledge and practices that emerged through the integration of medical traditions from Galenic (based on the teachings of ancient Greek physician Galen) and Avicennian (based on the works of the eleventh century philosopher and physician Avicenna). This approach to medicine incorporates elements from both the Greco-Roman and Islamic medical traditions, emphasizing a holistic understanding of health and disease. Bloodletting was one of the fundamental therapeutic practices in the Galenico-Avicennian tradition. According to this theory, blood was constantly produced and consumed by the tissues in the process of feeding them. Whenever blood stagnated somewhere in the body, or one of the other three vital bodily fluids, including phlegm, yellow bile, and black bile, exceeded and disturbed the humoral balance, a disease would emerge. In order to recirculate the stagnating blood and to balance the humors, a physician would remove the excess blood through bloodletting (Najmabadi 1974; Elgood 1951; Tajbakhsh 2000). The theory of bloodletting in Iran largely corresponded to the principles of bleeding elsewhere. In practice, however, bloodletting was not only a therapeutic option; it was even more widely and commonly regarded as a preventive measure. For many Iranians, bloodletting, at least once a year right before the beginning of spring, meant flushing out old blood so fresh blood could replace it and revive the body's general health (Floor 2004).

To the European eye, Iranians bled immoderately, and this observation bore a degree of exoticization that was not unusual in the Europeans' writings about the so-called Orient. For example, Jakob Polak, an Austrian physician, observed that "between the shoulder blades of all Iranians, there are scar marks." Polak first thought these marks were the traces of whipping, but later he learned that the marks were actually the remnants of wet cupping. He found the relationship of Iranians with various methods of bloodletting rather obsessive: "[Iranians] always ask the physicians: 'do I have blood' and it means 'should I bleed'?" (Polak 1865).

Polak was not alone in his astonishment about the immoderate practice of bloodletting. An English traveler in the late nineteenth century described the abundance of the practice: "In a morning walk through the streets of Ispahān [Isfahan], we have often seen the snow blood-stained, as if slaughter had been done in these public places. Sometimes we saw, in passing, the actual operation, a patient extending his bare arm in the street for the barber's lancet" (Arnold 1877). Such remarks, at times made in passing by foreigners traveling in Iran, were often accompanied by expressions of surprise and contempt. In spite of their projections and biases, these observations reveal the popularity of therapeutic bleeding. Depending on the diagnosis and the availability of methods such as cupping and leeching, bloodletting was widely accepted as a method to cure diseases and contribute to improved health (Floor 2004; Matin 2018; Nimruzi, Afshar, and Jaladat 2013).

Old blood was considered bad blood (*khun-e bad*) or filthy blood (*khun-e kasif*), and thus, presumably, losing it did not harm or weaken the body. Instead, letting blood was broadly understood as a euphoric experience. In aftermath of the practice, the bleeder would reportedly feel lighter, more balanced, and seemingly relieved of the symptoms. Unlike the ceremonial blood on the day of Ashura, the blood released through bloodletting immediately fell into the category of waste, something that was similar to urine or stool, whose measured discharge was thought to restore the general wellness of the body. A large body of medical and religious texts about the rituals of bloodletting provide detailed guidance about bloodletting: when to do it, how often to do it, on which areas of the body to do it, which vessels to target, how old the bleeder should be, what prayer to cite while doing it, and how to treat scratches caused by bloodletting. Yet, we never get any instructions about handling or discarding the drawn-out blood. From the point of view of the Shari'a (Islamic jurisprudence), this blood was impure, and thus had to be washed off surfaces. Dealing with spilled blood was thus seemingly similar to dealing with any other kind of waste. A few accounts suggest that this blood was abandoned in the environment, allowed to flow on the street in front of the barbershop where the bloodletting was performed, directed into a gutter, or gathered in a hole dug in the ground to measure the amount of the extracted blood (Rees 1885; Wills 1886; Wishard 1908; Elgood 1951).

If this blood was doomed to be dumped, if this blood was left in nature with no regrets, and in excess, the implication is that this blood was not desired and dumping it did not cause much anxiety. Its absence in the body did not violate the sense of bodily integrity. The fate of this blood was obvious and detectable, being left on the ground, trickling into the soil, or merging with sewage water. No one seems to have taken interest in this blood. In the context of bloodletting, not the blood as such, but the process of discharging it from the body and its consequent absence in the body fulfilled the task of healing. The material surplus produced through bloodletting was unworthy of attention and never deserving of reclamation.

During the last decades of the nineteenth century, however, an anti-bloodletting discourse emerged among the guardians of modern public health. The discourse unfolded at a time when high rates of mortality began to worry the Qajar state. Pandemics and famines had depopulated villages and towns all over the country, and the majority of Iranians survived into adulthood with bodies that could not contribute to the economy at their best capacity

(Schayegh 2009; Kashani-Sabet 2011). Similar to other modernizing nation-states, the Qajar state assumed the political rationality that we now know as biopolitics, to observe, record, and engineer lives and populations through medicine, hygiene, and sanitation and, therefore, secure the physical health and optimum longevity of the nation (Foucault 1984). Accordingly, the individual body, a unit that was essential to the functioning of society, had to be prevented from being fragmented and wasted for no good reason. Within this context, bloodletting presented a risk to the integrity of the body.

Figure 4.2: Nomad woman bleeding a patient by "cupping" (Weston 1921)

Bloodletting was also increasingly seen as a backward practice contradictory to modern tenets of biomedicine. The foreign doctors described Iranians as an anemic nation and blamed bloodletting as the key reason for this alleged widespread anemia (*ghellat-e khun, faqr-e dam*, or *kam-khuni*). In his medical glossary, under the entry "Anemia," the prominent Dutch instructor at Dar al-Funun Johann Schlimmer wrote, "a common disease among Iranians, mainly due to the old habit of bloodletting, which many Iranians practice before Nowruz" (Schlimmer 1874).

The criticism of bloodletting as antithetical to modern medical practice was likewise echoed in Iranian public discourse. In 1881, for example, in an open letter published in *Iran* newspaper, a doctor complained that many Iranians who practiced self-prescribed bleeding were actually suffering from disorders caused by excessive bleeding but these "desperate idiots" assumed that the cause of their illness was extra blood (*ziyādat-e khun*) and therefore continued bleeding. The doctor called upon the newly established Sanitary Council and proposed that the Council must strictly ban bleeding and only allow it when prescribed by a physician (*Iran* 1881).

Bloodletting gradually turned into a sign of ignorance and backwardness, widely condemned and even mocked by advocates of modernity both globally and locally. In 1921, a *National Geographic* reporter sarcastically wrote about a man who traveled for eight days with a caravan, searching for leeches for the bloodletting of a rich fellow in his town: "A peasant from Yazdekhast walked 180 miles and back to obtain some leeches for a rich and prominent citizen of his town, who was desperately ill." The reporter finished his observation by suggesting that the peasant's effort was unnecessary, for the rich patient "most probably did not need leeches at all" (Weston 1921, 465). While challenging the practice of bloodletting, the new discourse also promoted the idea of blood being of value, cautioning Iranians that their blood was a precious matter that they should not easily let go. For example, Mehrtaj Rakhsha, a women's rights activist, in her 1911 speech at the American School for Girls in Tehran stated that "if Iranian women were aware of the importance of blood in the human body, they would not make their infants let blood two or three times a year" (Rakhsha 1911).

In certain ways, self-flagellation and bloodletting shared the same historical trajectory in modern Iran. First, the subjects who practiced these two methods of scratching the body and extracting blood were unconcerned with their lost blood. The lost blood did not corrupt bodily integrity, and thus did not create much anxiety for the bleeder. This blood embodied pollution and had to be ritually cleaned and removed from the subject. Reformist discourses targeted both self-flagellation and bloodletting as backward and harmful practices. The unfolding biopolitics in the late nineteenth and early twentieth centuries pathologized the willful extraction of blood from the body and thus stigmatized it.

Conclusion

This chapter invited us to rethink contemporary techniques of bleeding in proximity and tension with the earlier histories that constituted the extraction of blood from the human body. We traced the transformation of debates around the extraction of blood from the human body in modern Iran and revealed how officials, experts, and ordinary people conceptualized blood in myriad ways. In the context of rapidly modernizing Iranian society, self-flagellation and bloodletting, two forms of cultural collectivity, were condemned as associated with backwardness and superstition. This chapter can be read as an attempt to historicize the body, and more specifically human blood, and as an exercise for pushing back against the essentialist ideas about the body as a merely biological unit. Meanwhile, this chapter is an early history of transfusion technology that intentionally provincialized the very technology of transfusion. This approach offers a model for revisiting the conventional chronologies and periodizations that are predominantly concerned with narratives of origin determined by stages in the development of medical technologies. This model allows us to come up with more inclusive histories of medicine and technology that acknowledge local stories.

References

Afary, Janet. 2015. "Foundations for Religious Reform in the First Pahlavi Era." *Iran Nameh* 30 (3): 46–87.

Aghaie, Kamran Scot. 2004. *The Martyrs of Karbala: Shi'i Symbols & Rituals in Modern Iran.* Seattle, WA: University of Washington Press.

Ameri, Ali. 2000. "Blood Transfusion Services in Iran." *Encyclopaedia Iranica* (online edition). Accessed in May 20, 2020.

Arnold, Arthur R. 1877. *Through Persia by Caravan.* London: Harper.

Azizi, Mohammad Hossein, Touraj Nayernouri, and Moslem Bahadori. 2015. "The History of the Foundation of the Iranian National Blood Transfusion Service in 1974 and the Biography of its Founder; Professor Fereydoun Ala." *Archives of Iranian Medicine* 18 (6): 393–400.

Calmard, Jean. 1996. "Shi'i rituals and power II." In *Safavid Persia: The History and Politics of an Islamic Society*, ed. Charles Melville, 139–90. London: I. B. Tauris.

Chelkowski, Peter. 1985. "Shia Muslim processional performances." *Drama Review* 29 (3): 18–30.

Dast-e penhān: Negāhi beh tārikhcheh, mabāni-ye feqhi va baztāb-hāye qameh-zani dar afkār-e 'omumi va resāneh-hāye beynolmelali [The hidden hand: a look into the historical, jurisprudential, and reactional aspects of blood matam in the general public and international media]. 2008. Qom: Bustan-e Ketab.

Douglas, Mary. 1976. *Purity and Danger: An Analysis of Concepts of Pollution and Taboo.* New York, NY: Routledge and Kegan Paul.

Elgood, Cyril. 1951. *The Medical History of Persia and the Eastern Caliphate*. Cambridge: Cambridge University Press.

Ende, Werner. 1978. "The flagellation of Muharram and Shi'ite ulama." *Der Islam* 55: 19–36.

Fischer, Michael. 2003. *Iran: From Religious Dispute to Revolution*. Madison, WI: University of Wisconsin Press.

Floor, Willem. 2004. *Public Health in Qajar Iran*. Odenton, MD: Mage Publishers.

Foucault, Michel. 1984. *The Foucault Reader*. Edited by Paul Rabinow. New York, NY: Pantheon.

"Gozāresh-e Jelowgiri az Qameh-zani dar Zanjan, 1930." [Report of preventing hitting qameh in Zanjan]. 1930. National Library and Archives of Iran, Tehran, Iran.

Hedin, Sven. 1910. *Overland to India*. New York, NY: Macmillan Company.

Iran. 1881. February 14, 446. Newspaper.

Kashani-Sabet, Firoozeh. 2011. *Conceiving Citizens: Women and the Politics of Motherhood in Iran*. Oxford: Oxford University Press.

Kasravi, Ahmad. 2005. *Tārikh-e Mashruteh-ye Iran* [Iranian constitutional revolution]. Tehran: Amirkabir.

Katz, Marion Holmes. 2002. *Body of Text: The Emergence of the Sunnī Law of Ritual Purity*. Albany, NY: State University of New York Press.

Lock, Margaret M., and Judith Farquhar. 2007. *Beyond the Body Proper: Reading the Anthropology of Material Life*. Durham, NC: Duke University Press.

Maghen, Ze'ev. 2005. *Virtues of the Flesh: Passion and Purity in Early Islamic Jurisprudence*. Leiden: Brill.

Matin, Peyman. 2018. "Khūn-giri." in *Dā'eratolma'āref-e bozorg-e 'eslāmi* [The Great encyclopedia of Islam], vol. 23. Tehran: Dā'eratolma'āref-e Bozorg-e 'Eslāmi: 255-264.

"Nafy-ye Qameh-zani dar Ayām-e Moharram 1312/4/3" [Banning hitting qameh during Muharram, May 25, 1933]. 1933. 293/38279, National Library and Archives of Iran, Tehran, Iran.

Najmabadi, Mahmud. 1974. *Tārikh-e Teb dar Iran* [History of medicine in Iran]. Tehran: University of Tehran Press.

Nimruzi, Majid, Gholam-reza Kord Afshar, Amir Mohamd Jaladat. 2013. "Moruri bar kārbord-hā va 'avārez-e hejāmat dar tebb-e sonnati-ye Iran " [A survey of the functions and side-effects of bloodletting in Iranian traditional Medicine]. *Faslnāmeh-ye Tārikh-e Pezeshki* 4 (12): 160–82.

Pinault, David. 1992. *The Shiites: Ritual and Popular Piety in a Muslim Community*. London: St. Martin's Press.

Polak, Jakob Eduard. 1865. *Persien: Das Land und Seine Bewohner. Ethnographische Schilderungen*. Leipzig: Brockhaus.

Puya, Yahya. 1954. "Hadiyeh-e Khun" [Gift of Blood]. *Ettelā'āt*, September 7, 1954, 1, 5.

Rakhsha, Marhrtaj. 1911 "Az Notq-hāye Fāregh-al-tahsilāt-e Anās-e Madreseh-ye Āmrikāyi." [From the Rakhsha's speech in the graduation ceremony of the American School of Girls]. *Iran-e Now*, June 29, 1911. Reprinted in *Women's World in Qajar Iran*.

Rees, John David. 1885. *Notes of a Journey from Kasveen to Hamadan Across the Karagan Country*. London: E. Keys.

Safari, Baba. 1992. *Ardebil dar Gozargāh-e Tārikh* [Ardebil throughout the history]. Vol. 2. Tehran: Mo'in Publishing House.

Schayegh, Cyrus. 2009. *Who Is Knowledgeable Is Strong: Science, Class, and the Formation of Modern Iranian Society 1900–1950*. Berkeley, CA: University of California Press.

Schlimmer, Johann L. 1874. *Terminologie médico-pharmaceutique et anthropologique Française-Persane: Avec traductions Anglaise et Allemande des termes Français*. Tehran: Lithographie d'Ali Gouli Khan.

Shahribaf, Ja'far. 2005. *Tehran-e qadim* [The old Tehran]. Vol. 2. Tehran: Mo'in Publishing House.

Tajbakhsh, Hasan. 2000. *Tārikh-e Pezeshki va Dāmpezeshki dar Iran* [History of medicine and veterinary medicine in Iran]. Tehran: University of Tehran Press.

Weston, Harold F. 1921. "Persian Caravan Sketches: The Land of the Lion and the Sun as Seen on a Summer Caravan Trip." *National Geographic Magazine* 39 (4): 465.

Wills, Charles James. 1886. *Persia as It Is: Being Sketches of Modern Persian Life and Character*. London: S. Low, Marston, Searle & Rivington.

Wishard, John G. 1908. *Twenty Years in Persia: A Narrative of Life Under the Last Three Shahs*. London: F. H. Revell Company.

5. Narrating Humor and Persuasion in Biological Safety Cartoons

CHUAN HAO (ALEX) CHEN

American scientists participating in the arms race of the Cold War faced a difficult problem of protecting themselves from the various chemical, radiological, and biological weapons that they were engineering. At Camp Detrick, the US bioweapons lab established in 1943, scientists at the Safety Division (or "S Division") created tools, protocols, and technologies to keep their fellow scientists safe from the microbes they were weaponizing (Vogel 2021). Led by Dr. Arnold G. Wedum from 1943 to 1969 (National Research Council 2011), the "father of microbiological safety" (American Biological Safety Association 1976), the group's efforts "became the foundation for infectious disease safety procedures, techniques, and equipment throughout the scientific and industrial communities in the world" (USDA 1977; see also National Research Council 2011). Indeed, conceptions of biological safety, or "biosafety," developed at Camp Detrick continue to inform the design of today's microbiological laboratories as well as how people keep themselves safe in successive epidemics like HIV, Ebola, and COVID-19 (USDA 1977; Cieslak and Kortepeter 2016; Covert 1993; Gostin 2021).

This chapter explores the theme of challenging stories in the context of the Cold War bioweapons laboratory, focusing on the efforts of the Safety Division scientists in creating a culture of biosafety where none had existed before. In the limited scholarly attention on Camp Detrick, most has focused on its role in the Cold War and the biological weapons program (Vogel 2021; Rosebury 1963) or the impact the Camp's microbiological research has on later biomedical research and practice (Lebeda, Adler, and Dembek

2018). This chapter takes a different tack by exploring the cultural life within the laboratory through a close reading of the *Safety Bulletin*, an internal document published occasionally (as many as four times a year) from 1952 to 1963 and circulated to all Camp Detrick scientists. Each issue ranged from ten to forty pages and discussed various safety principles and pieces of equipment. Specifically, this chapter analyzes the various cartoons, illustrations, and jokes in the *Safety Bulletin* that were used as a visual aid to break up the text and capture the attention of the reader. Close attention to the stories in these cartoons, positioned in the context of other Camp Detrick reports and the scientific literature at the time as referenced by the Safety Division, reveals the discursive techniques through which the Safety Division attempted to challenge (or sustain) the prevailing cultures of the bioweapons laboratory.

As conversations around masking and vaccination during the COVID-19 pandemic have shown, the mere existence of guidelines, training, and equipment for biosafety practices does not mean that people will adopt them. How to persuade an unconvinced public to take up measures to keep themselves safe is a difficult challenge (Overton et al. 2021). Scientists of the Camp Detrick Safety Division (CDSD) faced similar challenges as they sought to persuade their colleagues to adopt new safety protocols while working with microbes they were weaponizing (Wedum 1953). A 1953 cartoon published in the *Safety Bulletin* testifies to this difficulty.

Figure 5.1. Algae an Doc, Safety Bulletin 2, no. 1 (March 1953)

In the cartoon, titled "Algae an Doc," the first frame depicts "Algae," a young male scientist or technician (judging by his lab coat) reclining on top of a large rectangular clothing hamper clearly labeled "contaminated." Five Zs float on top of him, suggesting that he is fast asleep. Doc, an older scientist, stands near the entrance to the room. He points at Algae with his right hand and yells, "Algae! If I see you asleep in the contaminated clothing again I'll fire you." The next frame shows Algae still asleep in the contaminated hamper, except this time he has burrowed in deeper. Only his hand shows from under the pile of clothes, and he mutters, "Now for a good sleep. Doc, won't catch me now."

The two-panel cartoon highlights a real challenge faced by the Safety Division. Laboratory workers *did* sleep in the contaminated hampers, as the Bulletin's editors admonished: "It may seem rather surprising, and it is certainly foolhardy and against regulations, but it has been noticed that some individuals use partly filled clothes hampers (filled with clothing that is potentially contaminated) for a convenient place to take a midday nap" (CDSD 1953). Avoiding bacteria-ridden clothing might seem commonsensical, but Algae's insistence on sleeping in them shows that people have different "colloquial wisdom, judgment or assessment" of risk and safety (Geertz 1975). As Clifford Geertz wrote, not everyone thinks one should get out of the rain; there are some who hold that "it is good for one's character to brave the elements" (Geertz 1975). The Safety Division, as represented by Doc, wanted people to err on the cautious side. Whether Camp Detrick scientists, as represented by Algae, wanted to build character, did not think the contamination was a big deal, or were just plain lazy, the cartoon underscores how improving safety standards and equipment alone is insufficient to motivate behavior. Threats do not effect adequate behavioral change. Some, like Algae, react to surveillance by avoiding it and get themselves into more trouble in the process. What, then, is a safety officer to do?

Challenging stories like this still resonate in today's world. In one sense, cartoons like "Algae an Doc" are stories that illustrate the enduring challenges faced by safety officers and public health officials in creating a culture of safety. In another sense, short vignettes in the form of a cartoon are a distinctive kind of story that challenges its audience to change and adopt safe behaviors and practices.

In this second sense, I am interested in how the editors and illustrators of the *Safety Bulletin* conceptualized and sought to influence their audience. I see the texts and drawings in the *Safety Bulletin* as cultural productions that interact across the secured perimeters of Camp Detrick with larger social forces and shape a culture of biosafety in the context of post-WWII United States (Bourdieu 1993; Gray 2003). In using safety cartoons to challenge and reshape this culture, I show that masculinity was a key register through which the primarily male scientific audience at Camp Detrick was persuaded to comply with the new safety regime. In line with societal gender formations in the United States at the time, these challenging stories cemented a form of hegemonic masculinity that laminated safety with the erasure of women in science.

This chapter's argument unfolds in six sections. The first two sections discuss how the Safety Division framed their challenges in eliciting cultural change before elaborating on their strategies and tactics, homing in on how cartoons, with their emphasis on humor and visuality, became a favored narrative form. The third section uses the example of a contaminated laundry hamper to illustrate these persuasive techniques at work. The second half of the chapter explores the gendered dimension of cartoons as challenging stories. The fourth section shows how, contrary to the presence of women officers and scientists at Camp Detrick, the *Safety Bulletin* cartoons depicted a gendered dichotomy, depicting men as scientists and women as secretaries, wives, nurses, and pin-up figures. I then discuss how the text of the *Safety Bulletin* fashions its audience as male, highlighting how masculine sociality was the ground on which the Safety Division connected with its audience. Finally, I use another "Algae an Doc" cartoon to illustrate the role that women played in fostering this masculine connection. Where the weapon scientists' sense of masculinity was challenged by the Safety Division's authority, the Safety Division reinforced existing gendered dichotomies in the *Safety Bulletin* as a persuasive technique to show how compliance with new safety regulations would not entail the loss of scientific masculinity.

Cultural Challenges in Biosafety

In a 1953 special report on the safety program at Camp Detrick, Wedum identified two main factors that contributed to laboratory workers and scientists getting sick from the microorganisms they were studying: first, the inability "to construct, fabricate, procure and/or install known safety features and devices where they are needed in a reasonable time" because there were not enough people dedicated to these efforts; and second, the diversity of attitudes about safety, particularly among supervisors who display a "lack of initiative in safety, some failures to enforce or suggest workable modifications in safety regulations, some passive resistance to safety, and some failure to realize the extent and nature of supervisory responsibility for the health of subordinates" (Wedum 1953, xii–xiii).

As Wedum put it, these challenges placed "a grave burden on the Safety Director . . . who is given the hard choice of permitting additional illnesses among employees . . . or of ordering the stopping of these operations" (Wedum 1953). While military priorities pressed the safety program to adjust their standards, there were also what today's public health experts might term "cultural" factors at play: local values, social norms, attitudes, moral traditions, and practices that could "explain local recalcitrance and mistrust . . . [or] cultural barriers to compliance" (Benton 2017). In a 1964 article in the *American Association of Industrial Nurses Journal*, Wedum identified several factors beyond the availability of knowledge and technical equipment: "medical personnel as a rule tend to be more reluctant than . . . engineers or chemists to enter into a professionally planned safety program that involves critical scrutiny of the entire research process; and . . . there still exists a significant tradition of self-sacrifice, according to which the person in medical research is expected to be willing to contract the disease he is studying" (Wedum 1964). At Camp Detrick, this culture of sacrifice for both science and the military stood in the way of creating a culture of safety, one that explicitly asked the scientists to take care of themselves. This chapter explores how the Safety Division addressed such cultural barriers in persuading recalcitrant biological weapons scientists to change their behaviors and practices. Specifically, I focus on the stories that both illuminated and challenged prevailing attitudes about safety.

The Safety Division used a multipronged approach that included everything from new products for working with bacteria to reporting systems, vaccinations, and training (Wedum 1953). Wedum "believe[d] that work with infectious agents can be carried out with a reasonable degree of safety without undue hardships and undue slowing of work":

> The single most important factor is the attitude of the supervisor toward safety and his feeling of responsibility for the health of his helpers and associates. Many young men, newly elevated to supervisory responsibility, are careless in their attitude toward safety simply because they are too inexperienced in life to realize the effect of acute illnesses, chronic illness, and death upon themselves and others (Wedum 1953, 1–2).

What stories did the Safety Division tell the young men at the camp, like Algae, to convince them to care about safety? What tones did these stories adopt in order to capture their audience's attention? What concerns or issues were brought together to convince Camp Detrick scientists to change their attitudes?

If self-reported numbers are to be believed, the efforts of the Safety Division did make a difference. In the first decade, from 1943 to 1953, 340 accidents were reported (Wedum 1953, 3). In the last decade of the bioweapons program, from 1959 to 1969, only eighty-six infections were reported (USDA 1977, 152). This appearance of success is misleading, however, because infection rates remained largely stable from 1952 to 1959, for most of the *Safety Bulletin*'s publication period, until numbers decreased in the 1960s (Vogel 2021, 218–21). The Safety Division struggled in their efforts and never achieved the goal of complete eradication of accidental exposures. Yet the numbers only give a partial glimpse of the struggle to create a culture of biosafety. A close analysis of the textual and visual stories of the *Safety Bulletin* reveals the narrative grounds that underwrote the numerical data, illuminating cultural specificities that shaped resistance and persuasion.

Publicity, Visuality, and Humor

The first formal training program in safety and microbiology operationalized at Camp Detrick in February 1944 was a comprehensive course limited to officers and civilian supervisors who were in charge of their subordinates' safety. This was a full-time three-week course, but efforts soon pivoted to a shorter course of three half-day sessions for "individual[s] actually engaged in research and of the persons who in any way aided the research *man*" (Wedum, 1953, 37, emphasis added). This course allowed individuals to work and train simultaneously but focused primarily on individual safety. The content included "films [and] slides made of persons ill with diseases contracted while on the job [and] talks by supervisors and demonstrations of safety equipment" (Wedum, 1953, 37).

The detailed attention to presentation technique showed the Safety Division's recognition that getting people to take safety seriously is not as straightforward as reciting the microbiological facts. The division made their own moving pictures (with sound) as a visual aid for the training, incorporating the camps' own research data on worker hazards in the biological laboratory (Wedum 1953). Wedum himself wrote the script and the filming was done by the Armed Forces Institute of Pathology and the Public Health Service at the Communicable Disease Center (CDC, the forerunner to the Centers for Disease Control and Prevention) in Chamblee, Georgia (Wedum 1953). The Safety Division was meticulous about how they showed these films. They presented the film to nonresearchers like firemen and property personnel, arranged multiple screenings so as to not interfere with operation, held make-up sessions, took attendance, read the film summary before the showing to "focus the attention of the group on the film's pertinent features," and even encouraged discussions after the film (Wedum 1953, 40).

This attention to the mise-en-scène of safety training films reflects the Safety Division's concern with reaching a broad audience. Potential exposure to pathogens in a laboratory accident threatened not just the individual lab worker but also their colleagues working nearby, their supervisors, and the facilities personnel responsible for routine cleaning and maintenance. Addressing this heterogeneous group with different training, practices, and attitudes toward safety was challenging, and the Safety Division took several publicity measures to address their audience. Pamphlets, posters, regulations, and safety bulletins were deployed along with the films (Wedum 1953). In December 1952, dedicated Safety Division bulletin boards holding all these materials were installed in all buildings where sensitive research took place (Wedum 1953). The bulletin board was so important that it graced the cover of the March 1953 issue of the *Safety Bulletin* (figure 5.2). The Safety Division took care to install them on the "contaminated side of infectious units," where the scientists were handling infectious materials. Safety officers wanted to make sure that safety information was accessible to people in the areas most likely to need it and not filed away in an office on the "clean" side of the building (Wedum 1953, 43).

Visuality was thus utilized as a key form of persuasion in what William Vogel called the "moral economy" of safety, where the "Safety Division represented a threat to the professional autonomy of laboratory workers" (Vogel 2021, 234). Drawings allowed the Safety Division to challenge their audience without appearing heavy-handed. Moreover, the Safety Division needed to consider multiple types of workers, and posters were a key instrument used at Camp Detrick in 1947 to "popularize the practice of safety in the biological laboratory" (Wedum 1953, 42). The first poster simply featured various emergency telephone numbers, but it "proved so popular and useful" that it was constantly updated (Wedum 1953, 42–43). Figure 5.2 shows what these posters might have looked like, and the cover hinted at the contents of the issue, which included a discussion on laundry hamper design, the story of people sleeping in contaminated hampers, and the "Algae an Doc" comic in figure 5.1.

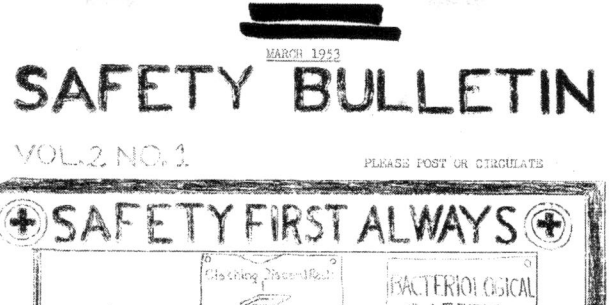

Figure 5.2. The cover of Safety Bulletin 2, no. 1 (March 1953)

The *Safety Bulletin* provided a forum for narrating safety in both text and illustration. Their precursor, a *Laboratory Hazards Bulletin* published in 1948, "was devoted to sketches of safety apparatus with information as to its fabrication . . . and was profusely illustrated" by Walter Duensing, a Pharmacist's Mate, 3rd Class, in the Navy

(Wedum 1953, 43; "Walter Duensing Obituary" 2013). He also illustrated a series of posters in 1948 "designed to make personnel safety conscious by the use of humorous art" (Wedum 1953, 43). The publication of the *Hazards Bulletin* became sporadic after Duensing was transferred to offshore duty, but the use of humorous drawings that he started was so useful that when the *Safety Bulletin* was created in 1952, Camp Detrick hired a dedicated illustrator, Fred Hammell. He created "Algae an Doc" for the publication (Wedum 1953).

Drawings and humor narrated stories that allowed the Safety Division to both challenge and connect with their audience in a more endearing way. An emerging area of research explores the potential of humor in improving the effectiveness of public health communication (Schumacher 2017; Cernerud and Olsson 2004). Recent scholarship in graphic medicine argues that comics can influence health behaviors as they "value the audience as non-experts and communicate narratives of lived experience" (Dobbins 2016). Drawings depict safety protocols in the context of everyday laboratory life to show what safety or danger looks like. The cartoon form draws attention in a *Safety Bulletin* that is otherwise filled with dry and wordy technical text. Moreover, the comic form (like "Algae an Doc") with its punch line allows the Safety Division to articulate the tension in trying to get someone to care about something that they don't care about.

Published in the final page of the March 1955 issue, the single comic panel shown in figure 5.3 is bisected vertically by a wall. On the left, a portly male scientist sits at his desk, holding up a copy of the *Safety Bulletin* while exclaiming, "Hmm, more safety! Nothin' ever happens to me. I need this stuff like I need a hole in the head!!" On the right, a carpenter is strenuously drilling through the wall, not realizing that his drill has already gone through the thin wall and is about to hit the head of the scientist sitting on the other side.

Figure 5.3. *Safety Bulletin*, 3, no. 1 (March 1955)

The cartoon form enables more complex social commentary. It allows the Safety Division to subtly signal to the readers that they are aware of how many folks resist the safety regime, but it also makes an argument for why attention to safety and safe practices matters. The obstinate scientist about to get a hole accidentally drilled in his head illustrates the cartoon's subtle "jab" at the reader. Humor is the non-confrontational satirical space in which the Safety Division can poke fun at their colleagues, teasing them for their foolishness. The cartoon positions the editors on the "same side" as the readers instead of an oppressive regulatory force. There's no vexing hierarchy forcing them to do something; it's self-evident why the bioweapons scientists should follow the safety protocol. If nothing else, they would want to avoid being the butt of the joke in the next *Safety Bulletin*.

The Challenge of Doing Laundry

In the tense, scientific, and mission-driven atmosphere of the Cold War bioweapons laboratory, it might seem strange that the Safety Division would be so attentive to a common domestic item like the laundry hamper (like the one that Algae slept in). Yet the familiarity of laundry might be exactly why more attention should be devoted to how people act around it. G. Briggs Phillips, a safety scientist at the Safety Division and Chief of the Munitions Division Safety Sub-section (Wedum 1953), devoted half a page of the February 1958 issue of *Safety Bulletin* to this challenge (CDSD 1958, 14). Citing an editorial from one of the most prestigious medical journals in the world, the *Lancet* ("Laboratory Infections" 1956), Phillips highlighted a quote on the utility of safety protocols: "All such precautions can lessen the risk, but so long as the bacteriologists wears the same white coat (with or without buttons) for work, for tea, and for an hour in the library he is falling below the standard which he preaches to the surgeons" (CDSD 1958, 14).

The white coat emblemizes the moral economy of biological safety. It is at once a potent symbol of medical authority, similar to the lancet (or scalpel) for the surgeon, and an ordinary piece of safety equipment, indexing both safety and the scientist's human vulnerability. A principal investigator with a white coat has complete control over his laboratory, but the white coat also shows that he is subject to the authority of the safety officer. While the white coat protects the scientist's body, it can only do so when used properly. Used improperly, such as being worn outside of the laboratory to a meal, the white coat becomes a vector for spreading infectious pathogens. To put on a white coat is to live in these complexities simultaneously. Safety equipment is only protective when complemented with proper protocols and safe behaviors. The message of the *Lancet* editorial is that scientists are humans, vulnerable to error and hubris that can turn a piece of safety equipment into an instrument of risk. A microbiologist who tells other scientists to wash their hands but forgets to remove his white coat outside of the lab fails to practice what he preaches.

It comes down, then, to conflicts between the scientists and the safety officer, as illustrated in figure 5.3, and between what the scientist *should* do versus what they *actually* do, out of habit, carelessness, or resistance. Feminist approaches to science and technology studies inform how these conflicts may be understood (Harding 1986). Scientists occupy specific gendered, classed, raced, and (a)politicized standpoints that inform how they perceive the riskiness of the world and what they do in the laboratory. Androcentrism also pervades scientific practice. To challenge existing behaviors requires a (re)shaping of the stories around safety in the microbiological laboratory. It's a difficult task. As Phillips illustrates with another quote from the *Lancet* editorial, "Experience in the industry has shown that unless the risk to be avoided is both grave and obvious most people prefer to believe that they are the lucky ones" (CDSD 1958, 14). Pathogens on white coats are not obvious. Scientists like Algae in these cartoons are prone to believing that luck, not following the Safety Division's guidelines, will protect them.

Phillips's discussions about laundry hampers, taking nearly a third of the entire issue, highlights the care that the Safety Division took to construct a narrative of safety (CDSD 1958, 4–9). After introducing the function of the contaminated clothing discard receptacle, the Safety Division goes on to explain why people should care about laundry hampers: "Although each individual discard garment may contain only a low order of contamination, the method of contamination has a cumulative effect" (CDSD 1958, 5). The editors dryly noted that the "natural tendency [of the scientists] seem[ed] to be to throw [their] discarded clothing at the hamper," explaining that throwing contaminated lab coats like basketballs can produce infectious aerosols. Furthermore, while "some of this potentially contaminated clothing finds its mark . . . much of it goes on the floor and is subsequently handled again," creating another exposure point. Rather than simply prohibiting the practice of napping in contaminated laundry hampers or throwing lab coats at the hamper, the Safety Division explained the mechanism of disease transmission, creating a sense of a scientific conversation between colleagues. Phrasing people's unsafe behaviors as "natural tendency" allows the Safety Division to avoid coming across as scolding, eschewing guilt in favor of logic as a motivator. Passive sentence constructions devoid of a subject erase the Safety Division's role in active surveillance: "It has been noticed that some individuals use . . . clothes hampers . . . to take a midday nap" (CDSD 1958, 5). The phrasing gives the impression that the Safety Division is a colleague giving friendly reminders instead of an authority with the power to shut down laboratory operations.

This strategy is reinforced by an exhaustive discussion of safety equipment features, the rationale for their design, and the methods through which their efficacy was tested. For the design of a new "discard clothing rack," the Safety Division detailed how the new ultraviolet decontamination feature was mounted and tested. Liquid cultures of bacteria were sprayed all over the laundry bag and the air was sampled before and after the ultraviolet lights were turned on. They then put the sampled air on agar plates to demonstrate that the air contained much less bacteria after ultraviolet exposure (CDSD 1958, 8). Narrating the scientific method, in other words, helped the Safety Division scientists justify their regulations and present themselves as scientists interested in the science—not the politics—of safety. Actionable next steps helped reinforce this story. A drawing of the new hamper design (figure 5.4) visualized the text and created an interactive opportunity. "Remove the attached sketch . . . and attach [it] to your work order [submitted] to the engineering department for fabrication" (CDSD 1958, 9). The Safety Division challenged their audience not by prohibition (e.g., stop sleeping in the laundry hamper) but by giving them a third choice beyond compliance and resistance (e.g., place an order for this innovative equipment).

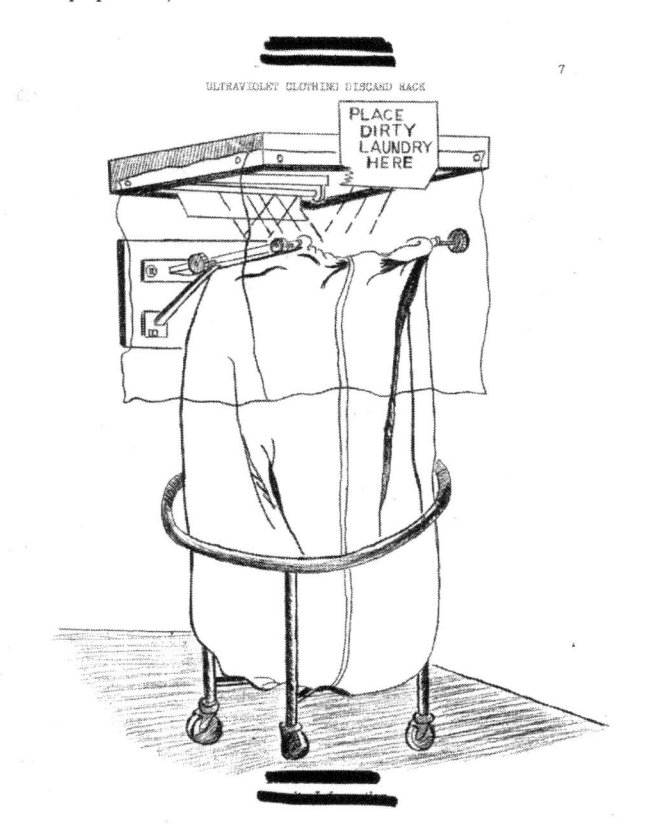

Figure 5.4. *A drawing of the ultraviolet clothing discard rack,* Safety Bulletin 2, no. 1 (March 1953)

Narrating Humor and Persuasion | 101

It's not that the Safety Division didn't issue dictums. But when they did, they avoided coming across as dictatorial by emphasizing systemic issues over individual wrongdoings: "Examine your clothing discard practices to see if you have a safe system" (CDSD 1958, 9). The challenging story of Algae and Doc (figure 5.1) showed that the Safety Division did not believe that commands, threats, and reprimands were sufficient to elicit cultural and behavioral change. Instead, the Safety Division portrayed themselves as passive observers, fellow scientists, helpful advisors, and even humorous colleagues to cajole the inexperienced "young men" of the bioweapons lab to take safety seriously. It was through these multiple techniques that the Safety Division challenged their colleagues to stop sleeping in contaminated laundry hampers and, more critically, to develop a new culture of biosafety where none existed before.

Women at Camp Detrick

Young men appeared to be the primary intended audience of the Safety Division. A closer inspection of the *Safety Bulletin* reveals a difference between how men and women were portrayed in these challenging stories. A drawing of a young male scientist removing his contaminated clothes and taking a shower (figure 5.5) accompanied an article that outlined the protocol to follow "in case of accidental spill of infectious material" (CDSD 1952, 7). The *Safety Bulletin* also featured a drawing of a male scientist donning an experimental ventilated plastic suit (figure 5.6), the precursor to today's positive pressure suits that have become symbolic of BSL-4 maximum biocontainment laboratories and emerging diseases (CDSD 1955, 16; Kasloff, Marszal, and Weingartl 2018; US Department of Health and Human Services 2020, 51). These illustrations helped scientists visualize themselves adopting new safety protocols, thus facilitating behavior change.

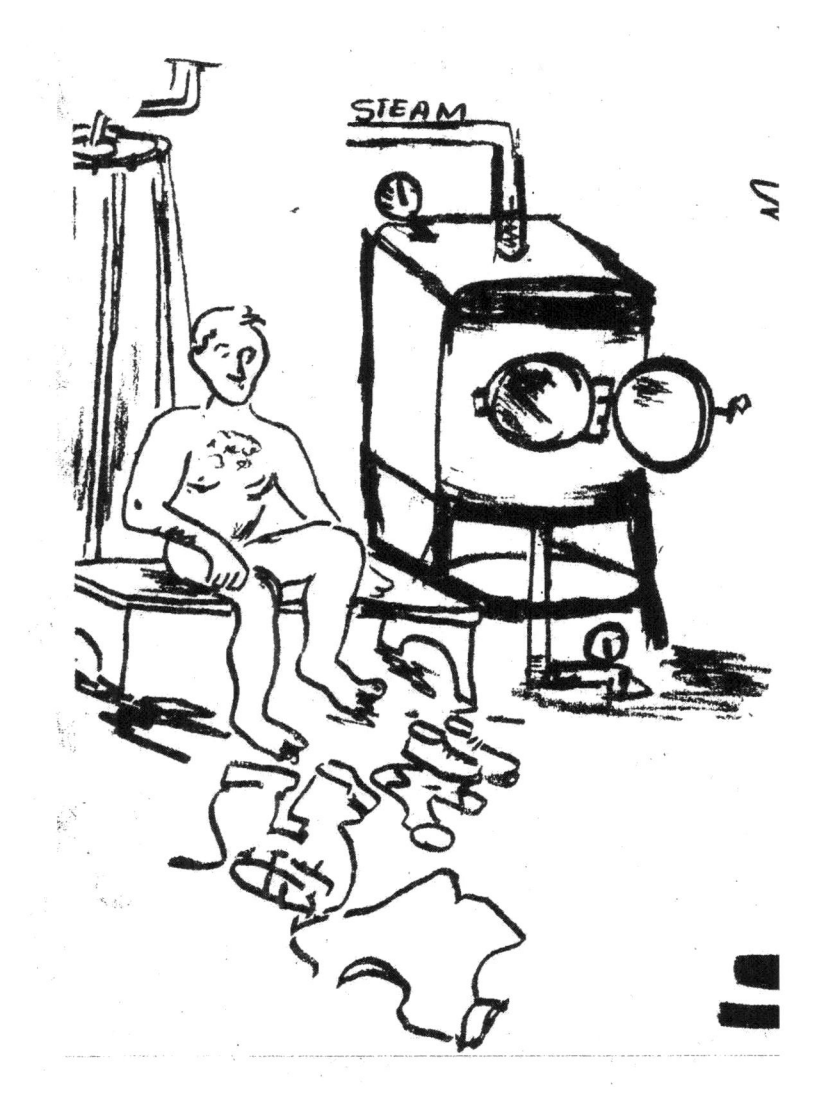

Figure 5.5. Safety Bulletin 1, no. 3 (September 1952)

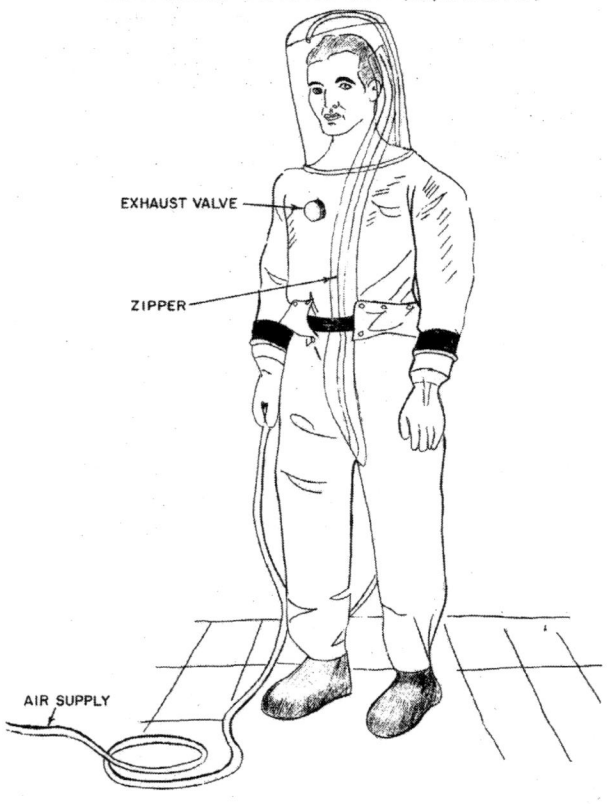

Figure 5.6. Safety Bulletin 3, no. 2 (July 1955)

The scientists in these drawings were exclusively male. In contrast, *Safety Bulletin* drawings depicted women as nurses, wives, and secretaries. A cover illustration from December 1953 shows a female nurse asking a male scientist with his hand bandaged for a form (figure 5.7). The March 1955 cover (figure 5.8), with the caption "If you are going to give blood!," shows a drawing of a female nurse drawing blood from a man in a lab coat next to the label "give this way . . ." and another drawing that shows a male scientist accidentally cutting his hand with a sharp lab implement next to the label ". . . not this way." A cartoon published in January 1959 included a drawing of a man entering a doorway, wearing a pin that says SAB (Society of American Biologists) and holding a bouquet of flowers and a rabbit stuffed animal (figure 5.9). A frowning woman—presumably his wife—greets him at the door. The caption says, "Thought you were coming back loaded with research ideas—!" A cartoon published in the October 1960 issue (figure 5.10) was captioned "—I'd like you to meet the safety officer's new secretary." This drawing depicts a woman entering the door of the laboratory, whose appearance captivates the engineer, the scientist working in the class III biosafety cabinet, the technician transporting two monkeys, the monkeys, and the rabbit inside the biosafety cabinet (presumably for animal testing), which has popped out of the hole where the safety gloves go through.

Figure 5.7. Safety Bulletin 2, no. 4 (December 1953)

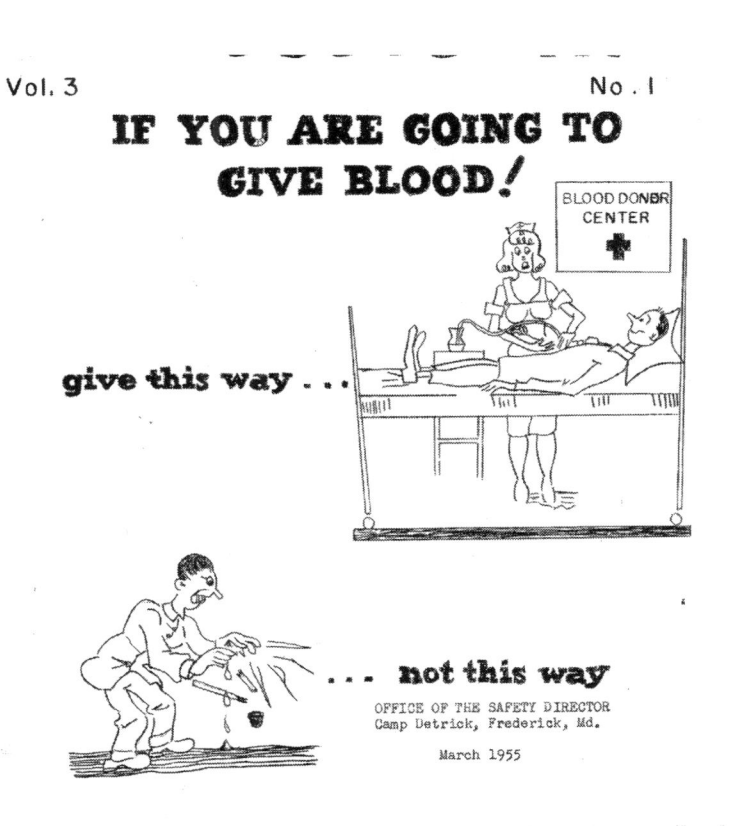

Figure 5.8. Safety Bulletin 3, no. 1 (March 1955)

Figure 5.9. Safety Bulletin 6, no. 1 (January 1959)

"----- I'd like you to meet the safety officer's new secretary!"

Figure 5.10. Safety Bulletin 7, no. 2 (October 1960)

What do these gendered depictions mean in the context of a military bioweapons lab? During the Second World War, the shortage of men in research labs meant that women scientists were recruited to fill the gap (Rossiter 1998). Newly created military services for women, such as Women Accepted for Volunteer Emergency Service (WAVES) for the Navy and Women's Army Auxiliary Corps (WAC) for the Army, recruited women scientists, including for officer positions (Rossiter 1998). Camp Detrick was activated in April 1943, and by August, seventy-one enlisted WAC had joined, relative to 328 Army men (Cochrane 1947). Eleven WAC officers joined 116 male army officers in November (Cochrane 1947, 76). The Navy took a more active role in the bioweapons program in 1944, and three WAVES officers (compared to nine male officers) joined in January, followed by forty-six WAVES (compared to seventy-seven Navy men). While the numbers fluctuated, the number of WAC officers in the army hovered around 5 percent of the total number of officers with a similar proportion among the enlisted personnel. Women made up a slightly increased percentage of officers (15 percent) and enlisted personnel (25 percent) in the Navy (Cochrane 1947, 76).

The postwar years, however, saw a rapid decline in the number of military personnel relative to civilians at Camp Detrick; whereas the military numbered 2,226 and the civilians forty on July 1945, by the end of the year the number of officers and enlisted military personnel had declined to 333 while the number of civilians grew to 174 (Cochrane 1947). This sharp decline in the total number of people, combined with the increasing proportion of civilians, likely entailed a decrease in the number of women at Camp Detrick (Rossiter 1998). The immediate postwar era saw a drastic reversal, with returning male veterans (as if women veterans did not exist), displacing the women who had filled the ranks of science during the war (Rossiter 1998).

The lack of female scientist depictions in the *Safety Bulletin* mirrors this shift. Wedum's *Report on the Safety Program from 1944–1953* named three women who worked for the Safety Division:

Mary Davis in radiological safety, Rose Lieberman in the aerosol Test Sphere group, and Dorothy L. Farley of antitoxin and vaccine development (Wedum 1953). The life of these "Hidden Figures" of Camp Detrick (Shetterly 2016), although they were white women who did not need to fight racism in their own careers, showed the disparate paths required for the few who were admitted to science's "Old Boy's" club (Rossiter 1998). Dorothy Farley (1925–2021), who graduated from Smith College in 1947 and Brown University in 1949, moved to Detrick for her first job and met her husband, who was a bacteriologist, and "retir[ed] from research in 1956 to raise a family" ("Dorothy Farley Jessen Obituary" 2021). Mary Shane Davis (1919–2004) graduated from Mount Saint Scholastica College with a degree in chemistry, served in the Navy, and ultimately retired as a chemist from Detrick in 1970 when she was fifty-one ("Mary Davis Obituary" 2004).

The one who "made it" to the top of the medical research echelon was Rose Lieberman (1913–1992), who has an annual National Institutes of Health (NIH) lecture named after her (Folkers 1992). She graduated from Columbia University with a BA in zoology in 1935 and an MA in bacteriology in 1937. Lieberman worked as a hospital technician and started a research career at Yale University, followed by work with the Veterans Administration and Fort Detrick. She then joined the Laboratory of Clinical Investigation at the National Institute for Allergy and Infectious Diseases (NIAID) and remained with the NIH for the rest of her career, garnering multiple awards for her pioneering work in immunology (Folkers 1992). She passed away shortly after the inaugural lecture in her honor ("NIAID Mourns Rose Lieberman" 1992).

Women also worked on the *Safety Bulletin*. Mrs. Phebe Summers illustrated the first few editions (CDSD 1952) and seemed to have been still working in a similar capacity at Fort Detrick in 1972, as part of the US Army Medical Research Institute of Infectious Diseases (USAMRIID) (DeRubertis and Woeber 1972). "Becky" Rhoderick and Shirley Brandt typed two issues each of volume 3 (1955–56), though no contributors beyond the editor were credited in the subsequent issues. Their names, like the importance of women scientists during the war, disappeared after the war. This continued what historian of science Steven Shapin has identified as the perennial phenomenon of invisible technicians in scientific research, where only the head researcher's name endures despite the research being dependent on a group's effort (Shapin 1995). It was difficult enough for women to hang on to research careers in the postwar era, and their experiences were compounded by the sexist "Matilda effect," the systemic underrecognition of women in science (Rossiter 1993).

Biosafety and the Young Men

The valorization of women at Camp Detrick was short-lived, tethered to the war effort, and paralleled what was happening across American science. Women scientists were minoritized in number and underrecognized, even on the pages of the *Safety Bulletin*. Looking just at the cartoons, one might assume that there were only male scientists at Camp Detrick. In both visual representation and narrative persuasion, the *Safety Bulletin* spoke to a primarily heterosexual (and white) male audience. The design of safety protocols, the explanation of safety principles, and the humorous cartoons catered primarily to his emotions and needs. These stories challenged the recalcitrant young American male scientist to behave and drew upon his experiences and perspectives to do so.

Indeed, the *Safety Bulletin* reads as a kind of male interest magazine. The second issue in July 1952 began with a line from poet Alfred Tennyson, "In the spring a young man's fancy lightly turns to thoughts of love," followed by this statement:

> Some of the rest of us being out of this class, think about baseball or, in our minds, visualize ourselves with a fly rod in our hand or riding about with the spray in our face. It's only

natural to dream a little but lets [sic] not do it on the job. It takes all our concentration on the work at hand to keep accidents away. Laboratory apparatus and shop machinery have no emotions, conscience, or sympathy. We must supply these. Think out the prodecure [sic] before actually doing a piece of work using apparatus that will show no mercy if not treated with respect.

What do the Tennyson citation and discussion about baseball or fishing reveal about the Safety Division's understanding of their readers? Who did they believe to be their primary audience, and how did this shape how they framed the argument for safety equipment and protocols? Historian Ian Nicholson has argued that the postwar decades were a time of "anxiety and menace," underscored by "a popular and at times flamboyant Cold War narrative of a seemingly lost or enfeebled American 'character'"—an enfeebled *masculine* character. Threatened by the rise of communism and feminism, cultural production of the 1950s mourned the loss of the "strong 'inner-directed' American male" and worried about the rise of an "'other-directed' conformist" (Nicholson 2011). Camp Detrick's Safety Division negotiated this tension between internal and external direction as they sought to persuade their colleagues to conform to safety regulations precisely when American masculinity was most troubled by conformity.

Camp Detrick is a paradoxical place in this context. As a military installation—albeit one staffed primarily by male civilian scientists—Detrick was subject to a rigid military hierarchy of conformity, one that was (and is) associated with national security and unquestioned masculinity. If anything less than "hard masculine toughness" was soft and thus a "threat to the security of the nation" (Cuordileone 2000), what did conformity to biosafety regulations mean for the masculinity of bioweapons scientists? Masculinity is not monolithic (Connell 2005), but the multiple contexts, structures, and elements of masculinities constitute a heady and confusing mix. How did the Safety Division play with these dimensions in persuading their "young men" (and not-so-young men) to take safety seriously?

Similar to the cartoons, discussions of love, baseball, and fishing became rhetorical devices through which the Safety Division connected with their audience. The use of "us" and "our" shows that *Safety Bulletin*'s footing is aligned with their primary audience, the young male scientists (Agha 2007). The shared ground of masculine concerns flattens the perception of hierarchy, but it also gives the audience the perception that they are the ones choosing to behave in a safe manner. Shop machineries have no emotions and will chop off a man's fingers without hesitating; any reasonable man would come to his own conclusion that he should be careful when working with such dangerous equipment. No safety officers—or their irksome regulations—are required. In other words, the *Safety Bulletin* created a narrative where the audience felt as if he had directed himself to these new safety practices *of his own accord*, instead of simply conforming to the external dictums of the Safety Division.

Women and Remasculinizing Conformity

What is the role of gendered dichotomies in the *Safety Bulletin* stories, especially in challenging the readers to adopt safe behaviors in the laboratory? This final section argues that the *Safety Bulletin* does more than invisibilize women at Camp Detrick. If conformity to safety protocols constituted a challenge to the weapon scientist's masculinity, then the gendered depiction served as a salve to this injury. The text of the *Safety Bulletin* makes clear that the primary audience is the male scientist, evidenced by four pithy jokes or platitudes that directly addressed a masculine "you":

> "A woman called the local Blue Ridge Bus Station to report the loss of a package containing a brassiere. 'What bus?' asked the BR agent. '36' came the proud answer."
>
> "You've reached middle age when your wife tells you to pull in your stomach and you already have."
>
> "When you take responsibility on your shoulders, there's no room for a chip."
>
> "There is no limit to the good a man can do if he doesn't care who gets the credit." (CDSD 1952)

Placed one right after another in the middle of a section on how to properly store gas cylinders, these jokes seem random. Each phrase, however, evoked a "facet" of the reader's character that combine to reveal the primary audience of the Safety Division: someone who is attracted to women; someone who is a bit overweight, married, and middle-aged; someone who has responsibilities and possibly grievances; and someone who wants to be a good man. More than boyhood daydreams of fishing, these jokes engage directly with postwar American masculine anxieties. The "good" of national security—the *raison d'être* of the bioweapons program—requires individual sacrifice for the collective good, including paying attention to the safety protocol. Manfully shouldering one's responsibilities to protect one's subordinates and colleagues should take precedence over one's petty resentment over the Safety Division's expertise and authority.

Moreover, these cartoons and jokes cement the bond between the Safety Division and its male audience. They are not just fellow colleagues; they are also fellow *men*. As Eve Sedgwick has argued, "the status of women . . . is deeply and inescapably inscribed in the structure . . . of relationships that seem to exclude women . . . male homosocial relationships" (Sedgwick 1985). The Safety Division's attempt to "bond" with their presumed male audience in order to get them to conform to safety protocols was bolstered by strongly gendered depictions. With women relegated to the roles of supportive wives and secretaries, as opposed to potential scientific competitors or even supervisors, the audience was assured of their masculine positionality in anxious postwar times. Jokes and cartoon depictions that objectify women served to create homosocial bonds over shared heterosexuality. This builds on top of the previously discussed strategy flattening the hierarchy between the Safety Division and their audiences: explaining the rationale for various safety equipment and protocols instead of simply prohibiting unsafe behaviors. Both come together to preserve the masculine ideal of an independent (but now safe) scientific investigator.

In other words, insisting on gendered depictions—men as rational thinkers and women as emotional caregivers—maintained a homosocial domain where male scientists can conform to regulations without losing their masculinity or their aspirations of scientific objectivity (Rutherford 2015). In these challenging stories, the presence of women would not undermine the bioweapons lab as a masculine scientific domain. Gendered divisions in the *Safety Bulletin* echoed the declining numbers of practicing postwar women scientists but also revealed the role of women in the remasculinization of men. Linker and Laemmli's study of the figure of paraplegic veterans from the Second World War show how "in post war America ... the 'normality' and performative features of the male body could not be assumed but rather had to be actively defined" (Linker and Laemmli 2015). While physicians testified to paraplegic veteran's masculinity via their ability to reproduce, films and cartoons of the era demonstrated women in service of that project as nurses and caretakers who motivated the process, accommodated male needs, and rehabilitated a sense of masculinity. The cartoon in figure 5.7 displays a similar process, with the female nurse asking an injured young man for his Form DA-285, the Safety Division's accident reporting form. She facilitated his recovery but also his participation in the biosafety culture that the Safety Division sought to create.

Figure 5.7 was the cover illustration, prefacing an editorial on the accident reporting system being instituted. The editorial described the proper procedures to take in case of accidents at Camp Detrick, including processes for seeking medical attention as well as the many benefits of following protocol. "The first person to benefit by an accident report is the injured victim. Regardless of the severity of the injury the person has established the fact that he or she has been injured in 'line of duty' and is eligible for medical treatment or compensation. It also gives official notice of the accident and/or injury to the immediate supervisor, and other personnel concerned with the operation of the division or section" (CDSD 1953, 1). In figure 5.11, another "Algae an Doc" cartoon narrativized this shoring up of masculinity.

This time, Algae has cut his hands in the lab and needs to go to the doctor. Doc checks out Algae's injuries, sends him off to the camp's doctors, and reminds him that "you are not to take injuries to outside physicians," because that would reveal the secretive work taking place inside the camp (Vogel 2021, 186). The next two panels show Doc grumbling at Algae's carelessness as he writes at his desk: "Now first I'll make up DA-285 as Mr. Hindman [the writer of the safety reporting process editorial] has requested. He needs these records in order to help prevent other accidents." These records were part of the Safety Division's surveillance structure, but they also motivated researchers to keep themselves safe by threatening them with bureaucratic forms.

A smiling Algae returns from the clinic with his hand bandaged: "Well Doc fixed me up. He sure is a great Doc that Green. That nurse he calls Grace ain't she a looker." Doc then makes Algae review and sign more forms. The final panel of the comic has Algae, standing in for the young male audience of the *Safety Bulletin*, coming to his own conclusion about the importance of safety: "Gee, Doc if I'd knowed [sic] it's all this trouble I wouldn't have picked up that busted glass out of the zink [sic]. I should have used forceps like you told me." Nurse Grace is not valued for her clinical skills in these cartoons. She is valued for her look, as in her pin-up portrayal in figure 5.8, as a soothing balm for injured masculinity. For the women scientists at Camp Detrick, this constituted another sense of challenging stories. These depictions not only wrote them out of the scientist's role but also devalued them as mere tools to support their male colleagues' bonding over science and safety.

Figure 5.11. Safety Bulletin 2, no. 4 (December 1953)

Conclusion

Figure 5.12. Safety Bulletin 2, no. 2 (June 1953)

In figure 5.12, we see Algae being distracted from his work by a woman in stilettos and a little black dress who suddenly materializes in the lab. He catcalls her: "What's the rush babe. Watch the hammer I'm hot to-day." Distracted, he fails to see that his equipment has rolled off and hit Doc, flattening him on the floor. This cartoon condenses the aim of this chapter: to highlight the role of gendered safety cartoons as challenging stories that facilitated the creation of masculinized safety in the Cold War bioweapons laboratory. Awash in concerns of national security, lethal pathogens, and midcentury masculine anxieties, Camp Detrick's Safety Division deployed an objectifying masculine gaze in their narrative attempts to persuade their primary (and presumptive) male scientific audience to adhere to their safety protocols. Women were depicted in a variety of supportive roles—as caretakers, distractions, and assistants—in maintaining a sense of individualistic American masculinity when it was challenged by group conformity to biosafety regulations.

As successive pandemics in recent decades, including HIV, Ebola, and COVID-19, have shown, it is hard enough to figure out the technical equipment and protocols to keep people safe, let alone persuade everyone to adopt them. Modern American principles and technologies of biosafety evolved from Camp Detrick, where safety scientists sought to address multiple cultural preconceptions and attitudes that devalued safety. With little data to work with, they tried to persuade recalcitrant scientists to conform through narratives. The *Safety Bulletin*, a widely disseminated internal publication about safety technologies, equipment, and protocols, is a rich source of these challenging stories. They illustrate how the Safety Division sought to intervene in the moral economy of safety, fostering buy-in through ample use of what appealed to their audience: drawings, humor, careful scientific explication, and gendered portrayals that affirmed their masculinity and independent scientific authority.

The cartoon, in particular, is a unique story form that subtly challenges the audience in ways different from written text. Illustrator Fred Hammell's "Algae an Doc" cartoon in the *Safety Bulletin* personified the main players: Doc as the authoritative Safety Division and Algae as the male bioweapon scientist, whose youthful hubris gets him into precisely the kind of trouble Doc wants him to avoid. Humor created a nonconfrontational space that allowed the Safety Division to highlight their colleagues' unsafe behavior. The cartoons flattened the professional hierarchies, presented the Safety Division and the reader as aligned in their goals, and created an emotional bond between the two in the hopes of soliciting behavioral change.

The context of American midcentury masculinity, one that was threatened precisely by conformity and the loss of individuality, illuminates how the cartoons navigate multiple power hierarchies. Indeed, humor and gendered dichotomy set a tone of homosocial bonding that reframed the relationship between the Safety Division and its audience. Rather than conformity, the *Safety Bulletin* suggested that, given the right data, opportunity, and stories, willful scientists will come to the same perspective as the Safety Division.

This discursive strategy, however, erased women scientists at the camp and cast women as props in the power negotiation between the Safety Division and the colleagues that they oversaw. As wives, nurses, secretaries, or even random pin-up figures who magically materialized in the highly securitized military installation, women were supportive actors who fostered scientific remasculinization where conformity to safety regimes challenged it. Gendered dichotomies as illustrated in the cartoons hid the complexity of postwar femininity, which saw individual woman's achievements celebrated at the same time that women were encouraged to return to the domestic sphere (Meyerowitz 1993). More importantly, this tactic of challenging one power hierarchy by reasserting another means that the biosafety knowledge and communications tactics that we have inherited from a half-century ago were designed for a very specific audience: the white male American scientists. Persuasive techniques of creating a culture of biosafety, as articulated at Camp Detrick in the 1950s and 1960s, fail to instruct us on how to reach those who were erased and neglected in the *Safety Bulletin*'s challenging stories.

References

Agha, Asif. 2007. *Language and Social Relations*. Cambridge: Cambridge University Press.
American Biological Safety Association. 1976. "Arnold Gerhard Wedum." 19th Biological Safety Conference program, October

18-20, Frederick, Maryland. Held in American Biological Safety Association collection, National Agricultural Library.

Benton, Adia. 2017. "Ebola at a Distance: A Pathographic Account of Anthropology's Relevance." *Anthropological Quarterly* 90 (2): 495–524.

Bourdieu, Pierre. 1993. *The Field of Cultural Production*. Edited by Randal Johnson. New York, NY: Columbia University Press.

Camp Detrick Safety Division (CDSD). 1952–1963. *Safety Bulletin*.

Cernerud, Lars, and Henny Olsson. 2004. "Humour Seen from a Public Health Perspective." *Scandinavian Journal of Public Health* 32 (5): 396–98.

Cieslak, Theodore J., and Mark G. Kortepeter. 2016. "A Brief History of Biocontainment." *Current Treatment Options in Infectious Diseases* 8 (4): 251–58.

Cochrane, Rexmond C. 1947. *History of the Chemical Warfare Service in World War II. Biological Warfare Research in the United States*. Vol. 2. Edgewood Arsenal, MD: Historical Section, Office of the Chief, Chemical Corps.

Connell, Raewyn. W. 2005. *Masculinities*. 2nd ed. Berkeley, CA: University of California Press.

Covert, Norman M. 1993. *Cutting Edge: A History of Fort Detrick, Maryland, 1943–1993*. Fort Detrick, MD: Headquarters, US Army Garrison.

Cuordileone, Kyle A. 2000. "'Politics in an Age of Anxiety': Cold War Political Culture and the Crisis in American Masculinity, 1949–1960." *Journal of American History* 87 (2): 515–45.

DeRubertis, Frederick R., and Kenneth A. Woeber. 1972. "Evidence for Enhanced Cellular Uptake and Binding of Thyroxine In Vivo during Acute Infection with Diplococcus Pneumoniae." *Journal of Clinical Investigation* 51 (4): 788–95.

Dobbins, Sarah. 2016. "Comics in Public Health: The Sociocultural and Cognitive Influence of Narrative on Health Behaviours." *Journal of Graphic Novels and Comics* 7 (1): 35–52.

"Dorothy Farley Jessen Obituary." 2021. *Frederick News-Post*, November 11, 2021.

Folkers, Greg. 1992. "Potter to Deliver First Lieberman Lecture, Apr. 27." *NIH Record* 44 (8): 8.

Geertz, Clifford. 1975. "Common Sense as a Cultural System." *Antioch Review* 33 (1): 5–26.

Gostin, Lawrence O. 2021. *Global Health Security: A Blueprint for the Future*. Cambridge, MA: Harvard University Press.

Gray, Ann. 2003. *Research Practice for Cultural Studies*. Thousand Oaks, CA: SAGE.

Harding, Sandra. 1986. *The Science Question in Feminism*. Ithaca, NY: Cornell University Press.

Kasloff, Samantha Beth, Peter Marszal, and Hana M. Weingartl. 2018. "Evaluation of Nine Positive Pressure Suits for Use in the Biosafety Level-4 Laboratory." *Applied Biosafety* 23, no. 4 (December): 223–32.

"Laboratory Infections." 1956. *Lancet* 268 (6948): 880–81.

Lebeda, Frank J., Michael Adler, and Zygmunt F. Dembek. 2018. "Yesterday and Today: The Impact of Research Conducted at Camp Detrick on Botulinum Toxin." *Military Medicine* 183 (5–6): 85–95.

Linker, Beth, and Whitney Laemmli. (2015) "Half a Man: The Symbolism and Science of Paraplegic Impotence in World War II America." *Osiris* 30 (1): 228–49.

"Mary Davis Obituary." 2004. *Frederick News-Post*, September 1, 2004.

Meyerowitz, Joanne. 1993. "Beyond the Feminine Mystique: A Reassessment of Postwar Mass Culture, 1946–1958." *Journal of American History* 79 (4): 1455–82.

National Research Council. 2011. *Protecting the Frontline in Biodefense Research: The Special Immunizations Program*. Washington, DC: National Academies Press.

"NIAID Mourns Rose Lieberman." 1992. *NIH Record* 44 (12): 12.

Nicholson, Ian. 2011. "'Shocking' Masculinity: Stanley Milgram, 'Obedience to Authority,' and the 'Crisis of Manhood' in Cold War America." *Isis* 102 (2): 238–68.

Overton, Denova, Selena A. Ramkeesoon, Kevin Kirkpatrick, Alexandra. Byron, and Esther S. Pak, eds. 2021. *Lessons from COVID-19 on Executing Communications and Engagement at the Community Level During a Health Crisis*. Washington, DC: National Academies of Sciences, Engineering, and Medicine.

Rosebury, Theodor. 1963. "Medical Ethics and Biological Warfare." *Perspectives in Biology and Medicine* 6 (4): 512–23.

Rossiter, Margaret W. 1993. "The Matthew Matilda Effect in Science." *Social Studies of Science* 23 (2): 325–41.

Rossiter, Margaret W. 1998. *Women Scientists in America: Before Affirmative Action, 1940–1972*. Baltimore, MD: Johns Hopkins University Press.

Rutherford, Alexandra. 2015. "Maintaining Masculinity in Mid-Twentieth-Century American Psychology: Edwin Boring, Scientific Eminence, and the 'Woman Problem.'" *Osiris* 30 (1): 250–71.

Schumacher, Amy Clare. 2017. "Humor in Public Health Messaging: Past, Present, Future." PhD diss., University of Iowa.

Sedgwick, Eve Kosofsky. 1985. *Between Men: English Literature and Male Homosocial Desire*. New York, NY: Columbia University Press.

Shapin, Steven. 1995. *A Social History of Truth: Civility and Science in Seventeenth-Century England*. Chicago, IL: University of Chicago Press.

Shetterly, Margot Lee. 2016. *Hidden Figures: The American Dream and the Untold Story of the Black Women Mathematicians Who Helped Win the Space Race*. New York, NY: William Morrow.

US Department of the Army (USDA). 1977. Washington, D.C.: US Army Activity in the US Biological Warfare Programs.

US Department of Health and Human Services. 2020. *Biosafety in Microbiological and Biomedical Laboratories (BMBL)*. 6th ed. Washington, DC: Centers for Disease Control and National Institutes of Health.

Vogel, William F. 2021. "'The Mighty Microbe Can Go to War': Scientists, Secrecy, and American Biological Weapons Research, 1941-1969." PhD diss., University of Minnesota Dissertation.

"Walter Duensing Obituary." 2013. *Atlanta Journal Constitution* (Atlanta, Georgia), Dec. 21.

Wedum, Arnold G. 1953. "Safety Program at Camp Detrick 1944–1953." Frederick, MD: Chemical Corps Biological Laboratories, Camp Detrick.

Wedum, Arnold G. 1964. "Disease Hazards in the Medical Research Laboratory." *American Association of Industrial Nurses Journal* 12 (10): 21–23.

6. Population Growth and Mexico's Production of Family Planning Short Films

MARTHA L. ESPINOSA

> I am Tiçitl, medical priestess. Among the Nahua deities, the closest place to the family corresponds to me. I was the one who took the bride to her groom's house by torchlight. There, I tied the *āyātl* with the *huipil*, uniting them in marriage, a decisive step indicated by the gods. I recommended the groom that his love be tender, and I taught the bride to take care of herself and take care of the fruit of her womb, prolongation of themselves and continuation of our proud race.

This introduction begins the short film A *Través de las Generaciones* (*Throughout the Generations*) produced by the Mexican Department of Public Health in 1976. As part of the national audiovisual campaign for family planning, this film uses Nahua iconography to establish a link between the precolonial past and modern Mexico. In fact, after this introduction, Tiçitl, the narrator, explains to the viewer that "the Mexican tradition of respect for life and love for children has not changed. Today's Tiçitls replace me, and they continue their educational task, valuing the benefits of family planning." The film depicts the new Tiçitls in the role of modern healthcare providers, nurses and doctors working at family planning centers established throughout the country as part of the government's new population policy, implemented in 1974, providing Mexican couples with information and contraceptive services.

    This chapter focuses on three family planning short films produced by the Mexican government. I interpret these films as an instrument to prompt the population to self-govern their reproduction. Relying on the definition of governmentality as "how modern forms of power and regulation achieve their full effects not by forcing people toward state-managed goals but by turning them into accomplices" (Agrawal 2005, 217), I argue that these short films sought to promote a new reproductive subjectivity among working-class urban and rural Mexicans. In other words, such reproductive subjectivity consisted of encouraging couples to have fewer children by promoting the idea that having smaller families would allow them to become middle-class and modernized citizens.

Historians of science, health, and medicine in Mexico have analyzed the different health campaigns that the government has undertaken since the early national period in the nineteenth century to improve the living conditions of the population and legitimize the state hegemony (Agostoni 2003; Bliss 2001; Cueto 2007). In many of these cases, the Mexican government relied on the support of foreign associations and organizations, such as the Rockefeller Foundation, to compensate for the country's lack of infrastructure and personnel to provide health services (Birn 2006; Cueto 1994; O'Brien 2017). This chapter builds upon such historical studies on healthcare projects, the professionalization of medicine, and the response of the population to the nationalist and paternalist healthcare campaigns. By using understudied family planning films, this chapter contributes to the history of medicine in Mexico by demonstrating another crucial form in which the Mexican state continued its project of creating a "civilized, modern and progressive" nation in the twentieth century (Secretaria de Salud 2010, 75).

Historian Maria Rosa Gudiño Cejudo has explained that health films have been one of the most neglected sources in the study of the history of medicine in twentieth century Mexico (Gudiño Cejudo, 2013). Indeed, accessing historical films presents challenges, given the dispersed, uncatalogued, and obsolete format of many of these films. Together with the National Film Library (Filmoteca Nacional), Gudiño Cejudo has contributed enormously to the effort to recover, catalog, and preserve Mexican health films. Moreover, United States institutions such as the National Library of Medicine have copies of such films that are otherwise inaccessible in Mexico. This chapter examines such audiovisual productions in the field of public health campaigns since they represent a unique opportunity to examine how different state projects have sought to inspire in the population, in this case, on issues related to reproduction.

In her groundbreaking work, Gabriela Soto Laveaga analyzed the massive media campaign undertaken by the Mexican Population Council in the 1970s, with particular attention to soap operas. The historian's analysis concludes that these productions contained moralistic messages that represented the "devastating" consequences of not planning pregnancies, such as poverty—and, because of it, mental problems, criminality, and so on. Moreover, Soto Laveaga explains that these shows relied on the common trope that depicted individuals who did plan their families as happy and successful, particularly when compared with those parents who did not plan their children and lived miserably. Inspired by Soto Laveaga, who has brilliantly analyzed the TV productions associated with the first family planning media campaign in Mexico (Soto Laveaga 2007) known as "Vámonos haciendo menos" ("Let's Become Fewer"), this chapter emphasizes that the Public Health Department produced short films as a propagandistic tool to convince the population to use contraception. The films on which I will focus for this chapter are *Una Mujer, Dos Destinos* (*One Woman, Two Destinies*), 1967; *A Través de las Generaciones* (*Throughout the Generations*), 1976; and *Sembrando Salud* (*Sowing the Seeds of Health*), 1979. To complement this analysis, I will also address the productions *Un Hombre con Visión* (*A Man with a Vision*), 1973, and *Planificación Familiar* (*Family Planning*), 1976. Although these two last films illustrate the official discourse regarding family planning as well, an in-depth exploration of them will remain pending for a future publication.

The films *One Woman, Two Destinies*, *A Man with a Vision*, and *Sowing the Seeds of Health* follow the same narrative formula. They present the fictional cases of urban women and men whose financial problems, caused by their large family, lead them to decide to use family planning. The main characters are rural and urban heterosexual couples, living in one-room apartments, noticeably tired and unhappy. Their children are dressed in rags. We see babies crying and an exhausted mother taking care of her children while also doing household chores. The dialogue begins when the exhausted father returns from work, entering the home where most of the plot will develop. These three films make clear that such couples are unfortunate because they are either ignorant of family planning, misinformed about contraception, or just too conservative and suspicious (either because of their Catholic beliefs or tradition). In all cases, the plot twist comes when the couples find an acquaintance, friend, or healthcare provider who informs them about the benefits of family planning and tells them where to get such services. In all cases, the protagonists take the advice, and the movies conclude with the couples attending the family planning clinic.

In contrast, the films *Throughout the Generations* and *Family Planning* have a more educational and informative approach. In these documentary-style movies, there is always an omnipresent narrator who explains three main points to the audience: (1) population growth is a problem for Mexico; (2) uncontrolled fertility diminishes the well-being of the families; and (3) those who attend the family planning clinics are responsible parents and citizens. To emphasize such points, these two films feature interviews with healthcare providers and include testimonies of couples explaining why they decided to plan their families.

Addressing the "Population Bomb"

In the 1960s, Mexico presented an annual population growth rate of 3.5 percent per year, considered by specialists as one of the highest worldwide. Mexican demographers used the results of the 1970 General Population Census to make projections, finding out that at such a growth pace, "the population would double within 20 years" (Ordorica-Mellado 2014). Unlike other Latin American and Caribbean countries, such as Chile, Peru, Puerto Rico, or Jamaica, the international agents that promoted population control and family planning had to maintain a low status in Mexico due to the government's pronatalist policy. The reasons for the Mexican government's initial rejection of family planning are manifold. In addition to the cultural and social influence of the Catholic Church, the government maintained the belief that a large population stimulated the nation's economic progress, particularly after the bloody 1910 revolution, which had a high cost of human lives. Such pronatalist state discourse extended well into the late 1960s, exemplified by the stance of President Luis Echeverria (1970–76), who, during his presidential campaign, famously asserted in 1969 that "to govern is to populate," which implied that that state's role was also that of promoting population growth (Rabell Romero 2021, 62).

Echeverria's pronatalism, however, seemed to drastically change in 1972, when he announced that the government would support family planning (Espinosa Tavares 2022). Although this change seemed to result from external pressures from regulating bodies such as the World Bank and the United Nations, who were asking the Mexican government to modernize its population policies in exchange for loans and financial support (Connelly 2008), the archival evidence suggests that the adoption of family planning was a process that discreetly started years before international pressure to make these changes. Moreover, by 1974 the Mexican government officially launched its family planning campaign, undertaking what the United Nations Population Fund (UNPFA) has considered one of the most efficient in the world. Mexico's National Population Council (CONAPO), in charge of coordinating the nationwide family planning services, received the United Nations Population Award in 1986, becoming the fourth laureate in the UNPFA's history.

In the 1960s, the production of knowledge regarding the consequences of population growth on Mexico's economic development began to spread across state agencies and permeated the spheres of state influence in Mexico, particularly as a growing number of Mexican technocrats educated in United States and British universities acquired more positions of influence in the government. Many of these professionals (including economists, physicians, and demographers) belonged to the national elites and distanced themselves from the more leftist and Marxist analysis of the economy and society that characterized Latin American intellectual circles during the Cold War. Mexican experts who endorsed family planning were drawn to the modernization theory and its byproduct, the demographic transition theory, which proclaimed that although all countries follow the same path to modernization, there are nations delayed in this process due to their high population growth rates, which are not in balance with the reduction in mortality. Interestingly, however, although Mexican demographers emphasized the country's "need" for family planning as a step to follow in order to "catch up" with demographic transition and make Mexico a modernized nation, they emphasized that population control alone would not fix Mexico's problems, so they followed Marxist dependency theorists in their call for economic redistribution (Fajardo 2022, 13).

As government advisors, these economists and demographers called for family planning programs to make individuals recognize the consequences of uncontrolled reproduction, while simultaneously highlighting the structural causes of economic inequality. The scope of influence of such professionals was pervasive at the main research centers in Mexico, such as the College of Mexico (Colmex) and the National Autonomous University of Mexico (UNAM), where they not only trained future researchers but generations of technocrats that later became state ministers and government administrators. In addition to organizing international conferences and publishing about unemployment and the economic crisis, these professionals developed national censuses, fertility surveys, and demographic projections. Archival records indicate that this transformation from a pronatalist or a populationist official discourse to family planning began years before Echeverria announced his support in 1972. In the case of the Public Health Department, programs to educate women on family planning and contraception were well underway by the mid-1960s. Physicians founded reproductive biology centers within public hospitals, and postpartum programs included contraceptive services as well. The most visible manifestations of the government's new commitment to family planning were the outreach efforts in the form of short films.

Representing the Need for Family Planning

The films *One Woman, Two Destinies*, *A Man with a Vision*, and *Sowing the Seeds of Health* feature characters meant to represent lower-class Mexican men and women, depicted as extreme versions of what would happen if they do not plan their families: they would be tired, unhappy, struggling economically, and living in squalor, with sick children dressed in rags and with obvious health issues. These representations were intended to allow audiences to project themselves on the characters, so they would feel compelled to seek public family planning services. In this vein, while the movies show the fictional cases of desperate couples whose financial problems are caused by their individual failure to prevent having more than three children, they also make clear that, even for those who already have up to eight kids, family planning would ease their problems.

Such a cautionary tale, however, was not exclusive to Mexican films. As a matter of fact, we can suggest that by the 1970s family planning films were a genre already established by the global movement for population control (Ahluwalia 2008; Briggs 2002; Bourbonnais 2016; Connelly 2006, 2008; Murphy 2017; McCann 2017;

Figure 6.1 The ideal, small, middle-class family, from A Man with a Vision

Figure 6.2 Inside the home, from Sowing the Seeds of Health

Merchant 2021; Mooney 2009; Necochea López 2015; Roberts 1999; Takeshita 2012; Winckler and Greenhalgh 2005). The worldwide population control movement started in the 1950s by philanthropists, eugenicists, and social and natural scientists based in the United States and Western Europe. Although the concern for population control was shared by governments in countries in the Global North and the Global South, the flow of money and technical experts to undertake family planning programs initially came from organizations located in the United States (such as the Population Council, the Pathfinder Fund, or the United States Agency for International Development).

In this sense, there is a robust historiography on transnational interactions between governments, organizations, and agents that participated in the population control movement starting in the second half of the twentieth century. Scholars have addressed the unequal relationships of power that the control of reproduction implies at the level of nations and international regulatory organizations, within the nation-state and the society, and between family planning agencies and the individuals whose reproduction would be "controlled" (see Murphy 2017; Ahluwalia 2008; Bourbonnais 2016; Briggs 2002; Mooney 2009; Necochea López 2015; Connelly 2006, 2008; Takeshita 2012; Merchant 2021; McCann 2016; Winckler and Greenhalgh 2005; Roberts 1999). Moreover, this scholarship has illuminated the complex ways in which neo-Malthusianism and eugenics persisted both in the ideologies of international organizations and in the projects born at the national level to undertake population control.

The fictional stories portrayed in the family planning films around the world followed a formula that compared large, low-income families (always seeming sick and unhappy) with small, middle-class families (visibly happy and healthy). The films proclaimed that the misfortune of low-income families was due to their uncontrolled reproduction. A representative example of this genre was Disney's animated film *Family Planning*, produced in 1967 in collaboration with the US-based Population Council. The main protagonist,

Donald Duck, helps the movie's narrator illustrate the threat of overpopulation to the audience. Tellingly, a "common man" and his "common wife" are featured in the film, serving as examples for Donald Duck to show the adversities people could face if they did not plan their families.

The Mexican film *Planificación Familiar* also used the format of a cartoon, thus inspired by Disney's *Family Planning*, to explain the demographic thinking that guided the population programs undertaken by the Mexican government and international aid agencies. Regarding Disney's film, historian Jadwiga E. Pieper Mooney argues that "Donald Duck appropriates the right to guide 'Common Man' and professes to fulfill a civilizing mission by introducing modern values and behaviors to far-off lands" (Mooney 2009, 72). Reproducing point by point the plot of Disney's film, *Planificación Familiar* replaces Donald Duck with a funny-looking, unnamed man who works as an interactive counterpart to the omnipresent narrator. This unnamed character supports the narrator by drawing his insights on a board as a way to visually support his explanations. For instance, the film introduces the demographic transition process with a scale the unnamed man draws on the board to symbolize society. One side of the scale represents high births, while the other corresponds to high mortality. According to the film, this balance between high mortality and high birth rates preserved a balanced population for centuries. In recent decades, explains the narrator, mortality rates have diminished with the improvement in health services, the development of medicine, and the increase in food production and its distribution. Birth rates have remained the same, however, causing society to lose its demographic balance. The only way to recover the balance is through family planning. These two films with the same titles, *Family Planning* (US, 1967) and *Family Planning* (Mexico, 1976), thus convey the same message: that modern men and women should alter their "reproductive behavior to create smaller families" (Mooney 2009, 72).

Interestingly, the family in the Mexican film does not look Mexican. The family portrayed looks more like a stereotypical white suburban family in the United States: the wife in this fictitious family is blonde, and the couple's two eldest kids are blonde too. In the Disney movie, in contrast, although the narrator states that they were talking about "a common man" and "a common wife," the seemingly non-white family could be from South Asia or even Mexico, thus representing a region of the world that was a well-known target for population control efforts.

Figure 6.3 A large family lacking in food, from Family Planning

The odd portrayal of a Mexican family in Planificación Familiar, however, was consistent with the media representations of Mexicans in cinema and television: actors and actresses, even today, are mostly white or light-skinned, no matter the character they're portraying, despite the fact that most of the Mexican population do not share these features. With this, the film reinforces the myth of *mestizaje*, or the idea that modern Mexicans are the product of the mixture of Spanish colonizers and native Indigenous peoples. This myth has worked to give the illusion of a "post-racial" society, while in reality, it ostracizes anyone who does not conform to this ideal, particularly the Indigenous and Afro-Mexican populations (Sanchez-Rivera 2023, 7). Moreover, as many scholars have pointed out, the notion of *mestizaje* has tended to idealize European culture and a white phenotype as markers of modernity, while maintaining an "anti-Indian" prejudice (Knight 1990, 10).

Contraception and Reproductive Subjectivities

In all the cases in which the films portrayed a family with more than four children, the characters lived in poverty and sadness. According to this reasoning, poverty results from the individual's inability to control their reproductive behavior, in this case, by the conscious use of contraception. The short films coincide in their use of the term "family planning," which serves as an umbrella concept for all the measures that couples could take to reduce their fertility, starting with attending the family planning clinics part of the public health system. Despite the state's effort to motivate Mexicans to self-govern and plan their families, there was still no open discussion about contraceptive options. The only film in which characters openly discussed contraceptive technologies is *Sowing the Seeds of Health*. This film also stands out from the rest because it is the only one portraying rural families.

In *Sowing the Seeds of Health*, we see different stories of characters that end up seeking family planning services. Among them is Dolores, a pregnant woman from a rural town who seeks medical attention from the community's health agent. By the late 1970s the Mexican state provided basic healthcare training to individuals from remote rural communities, with the purpose of extending the reach of the public health system in regions that did not have the infrastructure to offer medical services. As *Sowing the Seeds of Health* demonstrates, in Mexico, this model also allowed the state to promote its political agenda in communities that distrusted government's interference, particularly regarding aspects such as healthcare provision. In this vein, a health agent was a trusted member of the community that could also promote the state's public health goals, such as family planning.

Sowing the Seeds of Health depicts a woman from the community who also owns a little grocery store performing as a health agent. A few days after seeing Dolores and providing her with basic medical advice, the health agent visits her to check on her condition and talk about contraceptives. During this visit, the health agent asks Dolores if she plans to have more children. Dolores responds that she and her husband would prefer not to have any more, given that she is pregnant with her third. The agent, excited to hear this response, advises Dolores to take her husband to the health center to choose a contraceptive at her next consultation. The agent adds that because Dolores had some complications with her pregnancy, she may not be able to take the pill. While she speaks, the agent takes an IUD from her briefcase and shows it to Dolores, explaining to her that such a device will help her to no longer have pregnancies.

Sowing the Seeds of Health is remarkable among the other Mexican films because, in addition to discussing different contraceptives, it shows what one of them actually looks like. Considering that this short movie was broadcast in 1979, a year after the national family planning plan was finally approved by President José López Portillo, we see how the state discourse on contraception transforms from an abstraction into a very specific technological device for the prevention of pregnancies.

The only other film that mentions a specific contraceptive is *Throughout the Generations* when one of the women interviewed points out that she had used the contraceptive pill. This woman is the mother of another of the interviewees, Evaristo, a young man

Figure 6.4 Health agent in a grocery store adapted to serve as a clinic, from Sowing the Seeds of Health

Figure 6.5 Dolores holding the IuD provided by the health agent, from Sowing the Seeds of Health

who also shares his testimony regarding his experience planning his family. Following a more expository documentary fashion, *Throughout the Generations* presents interviews with experts and testimonies such as that of Evaristo and his mother. This short movie goes a step further than the others, however, by presenting the topic of overpopulation not only as a national or individual problem, but as an issue of planetary consequences. While this film conveys the same message as the other four (that uncontrolled fertility impacts negatively on the general well-being of the family), the film's omnipresent narrator warns the audience about the supposed link between the depletion of the world's resources and population growth. This last aspect suggests the state's adoption of the global population control movement's neo-Malthusian discourse that the Mexican government initially rejected.

Another aspect that the films emphasized as part of this new reproductive subjectivity was a modernization of parental practices, which also required the modernization of masculinity. The movie *One Woman, Two Destinies*, for instance, conveys the message that parents should not see their children as extra working hands, but as dependent members of the family that must be taken care of. *One Woman, Two Destinies* tells the story of a young Mexican woman about to get married. As she tells her friends about her marriage plans and they ask her if she would seek premarital counseling, she confronts a decision: should she plan her family? This leads her to imagine two possibilities. In one scene, we see her in the future as the poor wife of a mechanic, with eight children and living miserably. Her eldest son, approximately eleven years old, has to work on the streets, selling newspapers or even begging to support his family economically. The kid does not attend school, and his street friends convince him to smoke and steal. In the opposite scenario, the young woman imagines marrying the same man but living affluently with only two children. In this alternate reality, she and her husband are affectionate to their kids and seem to enjoy caring for them. These visions are enough to convince her to seek family planning services as soon as she gets married. As in the other short films, this plot emphasizes that couples should have only those children they can care for financially and emotionally. Furthermore, this film seems to promise couples not only the possibility of having control over their number of children but also posits family planning as a one-size-fits-all method to prevent poverty and instead become middle-class families.

The film A *Man with a Vision* insists on the need to modernize parenthood, with characters that represent new models of masculinity. Even when this film compares different families (the low-income family that "failed" to plan their children, with the one that did use contraception and was prosperous), it is interesting that the male characters are open in their frustrations and feelings and are willing to seek help. Simón, a poor worker with four children, confides in Emilio (his superior at the factory and a middle-class father of three children) that he has personal problems. Simón explains to Emilio that he has financial issues, his children are constantly sick, and his wife is pregnant with their fifth child. Desperate, Simón asks Emilio how he did well financially and had a model family. Predictably, Emilio's response is family planning, so he recommends Simón go with his wife to the clinic to receive information and prevent future pregnancies.

Perhaps more strikingly, *Sowing the Seeds* criticized authoritarian masculinity or *machismo*, an issue that the other films only implied but never explicitly addressed. In one of the short stories presented by this film, we see the case of Juan, a fisherman whose wife is about to give birth at home while he is out drinking with his friends. When Juan returns to his house, Mrs. Elena, the midwife taking care of his wife approaches him, scolding him about his carelessness in planning his family. Juan explains that the more children he procreates, the more help he will have in his fishing job, to which Mrs. Elena responds that this is an outdated belief. Moreover, the midwife tells Juan, "You only think about yourself, and you feel proud about having four children in four years." Mrs. Elena asks Juan to be more aware of the physical toll that four pregnancies have had on his wife, who we see lying in bed, tired and in pain. "Macho does not mean having too many kids," the midwife continues, "but giving them a good life."

Conclusion

One Woman, Two Destinies, Throughout the Generations, and *Sowing the Seeds of Health* were cinematic components of the government's broader population policy aimed at encouraging couples to self-govern their reproduction. These family planning short films reveal the state's efforts to address the so-called "demographic explosion" in Mexico by shaping the citizens' reproductive subjectivities in the 1960s and 1970s. By depicting economic hardship and strained familial relationships as some of the consequences of uncontrolled fertility, these films sought to persuade working-class and rural Mexicans to embrace smaller families as a pathway to modernization and a better quality of life. Moreover, the trajectory of Mexico's family planning campaign demonstrates the state's investment in modernizing gender (notably, the machismo embedded in masculinity) and social mores regarding contraception. Indeed, such attempts to modernize masculinity and promote the acceptance of contraception might have been the most transformative aspects of the campaign.

References

Agostoni, Claudia. 2003. *Monuments of Progress: Modernization and Public Health in Mexico City, 1876–1910.* Calgary: University of Calgary Press.

Agrawal, Arun. 2005. *Environmentality: Technologies of Government and the Making of Subjects.* Durham, NC: Duke University Press.

Ahluwalia, Sanjam. 2008. *Reproductive Restraints: Birth Control in India, 1877-1947*. Chicago, IL: University of Illinois Press.

Birn, Anne-Emanuelle. 2006. *Marriage of Convenience: Rockefeller International Health and Revolutionary Mexico*. Rochester, NY: University of Rochester Press.

Bliss, Katherine Elaine. 2001. *Compromised Positions: Prostitution, Public Health, and Gender Politics in Revolutionary Mexico City*. University Park, PA: Pennsylvania State University Press.

Bourbonnais, Nicole C. 2016. *Birth Control in the Decolonizing Caribbean: Reproductive Politics and Practice on Four Islands, 1930–1970*. New York, NY: Cambridge University Press.

Briggs, Laura. 2002. *Reproducing Empire: Race, Sex, Science, and U.S. Imperialism in Puerto Rico*. First edition. Berkeley, CA: University of California Press.

Connelly, Matthew. 2006. "Seeing beyond the State: The Population Control Movement and the Problem of Sovereignty." *Past & Present* 193 (1): 197–233.

Connelly, Matthew. 2008. *Fatal Misconception: The Struggle to Control World Population*. Cambridge, MA: Harvard University Press.

Cueto, Marcos, ed. 1994. *Missionaries of Science: The Rockefeller Foundation and Latin America*. Bloomington, IN: Indiana University Press.

Cueto, Marcos. 2007. *Cold War, Deadly Fevers: Malaria Eradication in Mexico, 1955–1975*. Baltimore, MD: Johns Hopkins University Press.

Espinosa Tavares, Martha Liliana. 2022. "'They Are Coming in So Fast That If We Had Publicity About the Clinic We Would Be Swamped': Edris Rice-Wray, the First Family Planning Clinic in Mexico (1959), and the Intervention of US-Based Private Foundations." *Journal of Women's History* 34 (2): 76–96.

Fajardo, Margarita. 2022. *The World That Latin America Created: The United Nations Economic Commission for Latin America in the Development Era*. Cambridge, MA: Harvard University Press.

Greenhalgh, Susan and Edwin A. Winckler. 2005. *Governing China's Population: From Leninist to Neoliberal Biopolitics*. Stanford, CA: Stanford University Press.

Gudiño Cejudo, Maria Rosa. 2013. *Educación higiénica y cine de salud en México 1925–1960*. Mexico City: Ciudad de México, UNAM.

Knight, Alan. 1990. "Racism, Revolution, and Indigenismo: Mexico, 1910–1940." In *The Idea of Race in Latin America, 1870-1940*, ed. Richard Graham, 71–113. Austin, TX: University of Texas Press.

Merchant, Emily Klancher. 2021. *Building the Population Bomb*. Oxford: Oxford University Press.

Mooney, Jadwiga E. Pieper. 2009. *The Politics of Motherhood: Maternity and Women's Rights in Twentieth-Century Chile*. Pittsburgh, PA: University of Pittsburgh Press.

Murphy, Michelle. 2017. *The Economization of Life*. Durham, NC: Duke University Press.

Necochea López, Raúl. 2015. *A History of Family Planning in Twentieth-Century Peru*. Chapel Hill, NC: The University of North Carolina Press.

O'Brien, Elizabeth. 2017. "'If They Are Useful, Why Expel Them?': Las Hermanas de La Caridad and Religious Medical Authority in Mexico City Hospitals, 1861–1874." *Mexican Studies/Estudios Mexicanos* 33 (3) November: 417–42.

Ordorica-Mellado, Manuel. 2014. "1974: Momento crucial de la política de población." *Papeles de Población* 20 (81): 9–23.

Rabell Romero, Cecilia. 2021. *Los Mexicanos: Un Balance del Cambio Demográfico*. Mexico City: Fondo de Cultura Económica.

Roberts, Dorothy. 1999. *Killing the Black Body: Race, Reproduction, and the Meaning of Liberty*. New York, NY: Vintage Books.

Sanchez-Rivera, Rachel. 2022. "Dystopian Eugenics and Mestizo Futurisms in Eduardo Urzaiz's Eugenia." *Bulletin of Latin American Research* 42 (1): 6-20.

Secretaría de Salud. 2010. *Cien años de prevención y promoción de la salud pública en México: Historia en imágenes*. México City: Secretaría de Salud.

Soto Laveaga, Gabriela. 2007. "'Let's Become Fewer': Soap Operas, Contraception, and Nationalizing the Mexican Family in an Overpopulated World." *Sexuality Research & Social Policy* 4 (3): 19–33.

Takeshita, Chikako. 2012. *The Global Biopolitics of the IUD: How Science Constructs Contraceptive Users and Women's Bodies.* Cambridge, MA; London: MIT Press.

7. How We See Ourselves in History

Stories of, by, and from Plant/People

MACEY FLOOD AND EMILY BECK

Plant/People is an oral history project and is one offshoot of a multiyear, multimodal series of collaborations with Minnesota-based herbalists about plants, health, and history.[1] These collaborations have taken the form of community courses, reading groups, study sessions, guest lectures, and extension classes, all of which have focused on exploring connections between history, personal narratives, professional practices, and experiences of health and illness. In the early stages of the COVID-19 pandemic, we were part of a small collaborative that was awarded a grant from the University of Minnesota's Institute on the Environment to pilot an oral history project on the relationships of health, plants, and place. After several pandemic-related reformations, the Plant/People oral history project fully launched in April of 2022, resulting in more than sixty full-length oral histories and interviews to date with people from varied social, cultural, economic, political, and regional belonging who are engaged with plants in pursuit of health. The stories that the Plant/People participants tell vividly demonstrate how the plants and land where we are located are fundamental to both community and personal health and healing. Through listening to them, we learn that relations with plants and land *are* health.

Our first interview with herbalist LuAnn Raadt in spring 2022 was in her living room in Northfield, Minnesota. Her husband Kerry was also in the room, where he would stay for the entire conversation.

---

1. Oral histories and short essays are shared on our website: z.umn.edu/plantpeople

They welcomed us with tea and a set of honeys that Raadt had infused with medicinal herbs. Interspersed with occasional comments to Kerry, Raadt described her childhood in a historically Mennonite community in Minnesota, her extensive gardens, and her Monday night group made up of students and colleagues. After we finished the interview, we caravanned a few miles down the road to a medicinal U-pick garden, which Raadt had started on a local organic farm.

Raadt's relationships with her gardens anchored our conversation. Though initially we connected with Raadt as an herbalist and herbal medicine teacher with a growing community of students and patrons around the Northfield area, Raadt explicitly tied her practice as a gardener to her views on health:

> The best way to get to know a plant is to take care of it. You learn how they grow, you learn back and forth. I think if the world could be perfect in my eyes, everybody would grow and make their own medicine and never come to me, but that's not practical. . . . I just think if you grow something you have had that personal impact, you and the plant have been back and forth. You take care of the plant. The plant takes care of you. Best medicine you can make (Raadt 2022).

Raadt's perspective on health, that the "best medicine" was produced through the "back and forth" of caretaking between humans and plants, would be echoed by many other participants we interviewed.

We began Plant/People by connecting with and interviewing people we knew: first our herbal teachers, then others in the Twin Cities metro area whom people we trusted identified as practicing health through their relationships with plants and land. We have prioritized developing a research network through relationships, a practice we want to name as having been learned through participation in Indigenous Studies academic scholarship, spaces held by Indigenous scholars, our conversations with Plant/People participants, and teachers at the Cultural Wellness Center in south

Minneapolis. We have asked each participant who they think we should speak to next, and we reach out to potential participants only at the recommendation of others. This modality has been slow-moving. Though it risks insularity, as there are many people and peoples we will not meet, it invites participants to shape the project's scope, and it integrates accountability between researchers and participants into the research design. This last point is crucial. Although we each practice health through plants in different ways, we are through our social, cultural, and institutional identities often "outsiders" to those with whom we speak. The Plant/People interviews have taken on the shape of an organic network of community relationships that in some ways intertwine with our own but in other ways are entirely new to us.

Our interview methodology has been to be as open-ended as possible. We offer our participants a set of basic questions on their relationship to plants, land, and health over the course of their lives, but we ask them to direct the conversation to moments and themes in their past and present that they most want to have held, as it were, in the historical record. While we are all participants in the conversation, it is, after all, their story, and the people with whom we speak and the questions that we ask are ultimately collaborative efforts between ourselves and project participants. Good relationships are essential to the goals of this project: listening to and recording stories, together, to build capacity toward a healthier way of being on land and with each other.

If there is one principal finding from this project, it would be, as articulated by Raadt, "You take care of the plant. The plant takes care of you." In the interview cited above, Raadt articulated the critical importance of relationships between humans and more-than-humans in general health maintenance as well as healing from illness. In these interviews, affective relationships between humans and plants are a frequent, even primary theme within the stories told by individuals who identify themselves and others as "plant people." In stories of their lives and practices, participants often speak to their everyday relationships with plants as teachers, mentors, kin, and friends. A common denominator in participants' conversations, and the way they recognize each other and themselves in this project and beyond, is a set of resonant worldviews in which plants are integrated into health practices not as mechanics or resources toward health, but as active participants and part of an everyday fabric of health itself. These oral histories are rarely stories about using individual plants as medical solutions. They are records of deep, consistent, even radical relationships across time between diverse people and plants—and land, water, animals, and other beings of the so-called natural world—one consequence of which is physical and social health (Geniusz 2015; Horn, Kimmerer, and Hausdoerffer 2021; Kimmerer 2013; Simpson 2011).

Participants' stories are powerful and distinct. Like people, they can be contradictory or unsettling. Some include images or moments that are hard to talk about and listen to. To speak to the theme of this volume, these stories are challenging in ways that are extraordinarily complex and deeply rooted in history, from racism and bodily trauma to mental health struggles and experiences with unjust laws and policies. Participants discuss rupture and loss, often side by side with stories about resilience and transformation. The Plant/People interviews demonstrate how radical relationships between people and the more-than-human world can build and reinvigorate community and offer support and strength in times of difficulty. The Plant/People interviews prompt us to challenge our own research practices. In the words of one participant, "To whom or to what is this work in service?"

Reckoning with History and the Land

Plant/People centers plant health practitioners in and around Bde Óta Othúŋwe (Village of Many Lakes) and Imnížaska Othúŋwe (Village along the White Cliffs), where the Wakpá Tháŋka

(Mississippi River) and Mnísota Wakpá (Minnesota River) come together in a place called Bdote in Dakota language. This area is also called the Twin Cities of Minneapolis and Saint Paul, Minnesota. Dakota people recognize this as sacred territory, a territory of origin. This area is also boundary territory, where other Indigenous people including Anishinaabeg traded, lived, and raised families for generations.

This region is also a place of deep Black roots, such as the fur trader Pierre Bonga, who married into Ojibwe kin in the north; Harriet Robinson and Dred Scott, held in slavery at the fort built at Bdote; and the families who moved to the Twin Cities during the Great Migration and built the thriving economic and social center of the Rondo area of St. Paul. These places are marked by settler colonialism and racism and their ever-unfolding consequences: redlined neighborhoods, a highway disrupting a historically Black business district, and contemporary environmental justice concerns. Finally, this is a place of multiple migrations. Scandinavian foresters, Bohemian housewives, Hmong farmers, and West African restaurateurs have made homes here, some in places that no longer exist. This region has a wealth of institutions and individuals practicing health in non-biomedical ways, many of which are based on relations with plants.

The relatively contemporary acceptance of plant-based health practices in the Twin Cities, and in the United States more broadly, belies their long-standing suppression. Culturally specific health practices including botanical medicines have been subject to generations of legal and cultural oppression (Flood and Myhal 2022). Multiple convergent factors have rendered and continue to render many nonbiomedical practices inaccessible, inoperable, discouraged, repressed, or outright prohibited. These histories are old and complicated, dating to early convergences of European and African descended peoples with Indigenous nations of Turtle Island (Schiebinger 2007; Wisecup 2013; Geniusz 2015). Individuals, primarily but not exclusively white, seeking land, power, and resources oppressed or suppressed the health practices of communities of African and Indigenous descent through kidnapping, forced migration, family separation, community destruction, and criminalization (Cameron, Kelton, and Swedlund 2015; Fett 2002). The United States government as well as religious organizations targeted the medicinal practices of Indigenous nations, even as plant-based health practices were practiced between Indigenous and settler communities, and enslaved African and Indigenous healers often played a significant role in medical systems accessed by white people (Fett 2002).

As doctors professionalized and established legal control over the medical marketplace in the United States in the late nineteenth century, economic and legal marginalization of plant-specific practices crystallized (Gabriel 2019; Flannery and Berman 2001; Philpott and Crellin 1990; Whorton 2002). The pharmaceutical and medical professions continued to prioritize plant-based medicine, but the acceptable location of these practices transitioned into the laboratory. Many social and cultural groups continued to integrate plants into health practices, but professional physicians and the medico-legal community ejected home-based and non-laboratory-based plant medicine from legal protection, professional recognition, and ultimately broad acceptance. Many herbal practitioners from varied national, racial, religious, and regional identities hid their practices or operated outside of more visible social, economic, and political centers, offering services, treatments, and training in secret or with altered language that did not highlight the medical nature of their labors. These legal and social shifts marginalized herbal practices along racial, class, and ethnic lines.

This social marginalization of botanical practices meant that when the popular acceptance of many non-biomedical health practices including the use of plants resurged in the 1960s, stories about the "herbal renaissance" often privileged the perspectives of a few popular practitioners, typically but not solely white, male, and middle-class, and often from the West and East coasts of the United States (Armbrecht 2021; Dougherty 2005; Griggs 1997). As with many histories, the voices that are most privileged in a culture are those whose stories are allowed to be heard. Overt and inadvertent sexism, racism, xenophobia, and regional biases, along with legal structures that depend on state governments, have meant that certain communities' plant medicine narratives have been kept from internal as well as public awareness, although some communities might not have wished to have their practices put on view in the first place (Geniusz 2015). A few potential participants, for example, have shared with us that they will not participate in the project because their herbal health knowledge is sacred and not meant to be shared outside of their communities. That the history of herbalism and other plant-based health practices has been defined largely by a few nonrepresentative practitioners is a strong motivator for our project, which amplifies stories of those whose voices have not been privileged with the goal of telling a more complete history of this movement.

Many participants have emphasized spiritual and cultural valences of health as essentially interconnected. One of these was Cheré Bergeron. As is typical to our process, we initiated the interview by stating the time, date, and our locations, then handed it over to Bergeron. They opened both oral history interviews by describing the time of day and year using multiple calendar systems, noting the Gregorian date as well as the lunar month in Dakota, Ojibwe, and Norse knowledge traditions:

> It is March 8th, 2022, on the Gregorian calendar, same time as y'all mentioned and ... the month ... or the moon time that we're in right now, in Dakota tradition it's Sore Eyes Moon, the moon of March. So the sun is really bright at times and it glistens and shines on the snow that it can actually be blinding. And then in Ojibwe tradition, it's called Snow Crust Moon. So we've got kind of that snow that has that crust on it. Some of the last, one of the last snow months, I think, that we have. And in the tradition of some of my ancestors, the moon in March is associated with birch trees,

with snow spirits, and also with "blythe," which is a word and also healing spirit in Norse root tradition that is associated with joy, lightness, levity, and laughter. (Bergeron 2022)

Bergeron then described their location—their home apothecary in Minneapolis—and the candles they had lit on their altar. When we asked them about their upbringing, Bergeron responded with emotion: "Even just being asked that question. It just brings up so much for me ... I'm here by way of my ancestors and I'm so honored to acknowledge them ... I also feel ... the weight of the responsibility that comes with that honoring. And I haven't been asked to speak about them in a while ... I think I'm just kind of feeling them coming to be with me. ... Uffda, we say" (Bergeron 2022). In describing their contemporary relations with their ancestors, Bergeron invited their presence into the conversation. The ensuing interview meandered through Bergeron's experiences with plants at different points in their life, to the people and texts from whom they learned herbalism, to the many modalities of their healing practice. At many points, Bergeron described how important it was to them that their practices with plants were a means by which they could address and embody culturally specific practices—that is, specific to their European ancestry. They were also a means to address the people of the places where they live. Using cultural specificity when naming the phases of the moon, for example, was one way they sought to use narrative regarding their relations with the natural world to repair, or heal, historical wrongs. At the close of the oral history, Bergeron thanked us for listening. "Stories are medicine, right? ... Like, this is a form of medicine right now" (Bergeron 2022).

The diversity of the ways Plant/People participants focus on and practice health with plants means that their stories illuminate a geography of relationships between people, plants, and land that highlight how health is intrinsically tied to each participant's cosmology, or way of understanding how the world works. Participants point to a multidimensional nature with which plants and land are integrated into their lives in ways that look very little like medicine and are very much about health. Most participants do not primarily identify using the phrase "plant people," but rather they identify as herbalists, gardeners, artists, or activists or by other social, cultural, ethnic, or political identifiers. The descriptor "plant people" is one the authors have distilled as shorthand for individuals who recognize themselves and others as described below. When describing the project and participants, we have found the phrase "plant people" and the manner of its use commonly agreeable to participants.

Community Healing: Plants and Land as Health

Donyelle Headington is a *völva* (cultural leader in the Nordic tradition) and herbalist of mixed African and European descent. Like Raadt, Headington is a gardener; like Bergeron, Headington is a culture worker; for all of them, "herbalism," or the specific practice of herbs as medicine, is but one of many interlocking practices aimed at health. We met at Headington's home. At the table, Headington had set down a plate of cucumbers with salt and vinegar, a plate of Lorna Doone cookies, and a pitcher of limeade with lemon balm from her garden. The refreshments that Headington offered us were intentional; the cucumbers were a favored summer snack in her family. About the cookies, Headington said, "I use them for my ancestor altars and I encourage other people to, because it was kind of like the fancy shortbread cookie for early America... So they're easy to come by to put on the ancestor altars. They remind me of my ... grandmothers, so I always have Lorna Doones, and these actually came from Mother Atum's house" (Headington 2022). Atum Azzahir is one of Headington's cultural teachers and elders, so these cookies were particularly special. Although our conversation with Headington was filled with laughter and fun, elements of the way Headington hosted us were evidence of the gravity of the conversation and seriousness with which Headington approached her own familial and cultural history.

Headington was born and raised in North Minneapolis, where, in her words, her family was always moving to "escape deep poverty." A self-professed "weed eater," Headington primarily learned to forage from her father, Jerry, who had grown up in rural Mississippi and would purportedly sometimes fish for his breakfast before school. For Headington, "weed eating" was a practice born from necessity, familial values, and play. Her father made wine from dandelions and wild grapes to build his blood in the winter, a health practice embedded within many African American communities. Headington was frequently sick with asthma as a child, and, as she recalls, the remedies of doctors in hospitals were less effective by miles than the herbal teas her father snuck to her bedside. Until his passing, her father continued to give Headington advice about ways to build her blood and be healthy by turning to plants.

Indeed, Headington's deep faith in her father Jerry's integrity, as she explained it to us, was represented in large part by his commitment to living in close relationship with the land. After experiences of violent workplace racism and displacement due to gentrification, her father made a concerted effort to go off the grid and rely on the land for sustenance both physical and spiritual:

> He won't contribute to a society that he feels like is not . . . He lives really on his own terms. And he won't do anything that jeopardizes his integrity. He just won't. And so that is, I would say, a significant piece of him living the way he does. And then the other piece is he just really enjoys himself. Like he's, it's like an adventure every day for him (Headington 2022).

Gardening, foraging, even setting an intentional table are thus components of healthy ways of being in the world. Headington and her father create physical and cultural health through relations with plants. The lemon balm she served to us in the limeade was just one example. Lemon balm is an herb that she has brought to place upon tables in racial reconciliation workshops. Its role has been as relational support for challenging conversations—in her words, "Please just take a piece and shove it in your nostrils when you feel like you're gonna freak out." At the end of the conversation, Headington returned to the ways in which plant relationships help people deal with being in time, calling this healing: "I think that for certain people, being a part of the kind of cycles and rotations and process of being in the garden or being with the earth and being with the plants is like healing, you know, like it kind of puts you outside of everything that's going on in the moment, which is really just a moment" (Headington 2022).

As historians of medicine, we must recognize that history is embedded in the ways in which people practice healthcare in the world. Understanding that a community knows its own history has meant that we must accept how participants will guide us. Through the conversations that create oral histories, plant-based health practitioners have articulated how their practices have been and continue to be affected by historical forces and events. They are working with their histories as part of being in partnership with plants in pursuit of health. Tim Clemens, a professional forager, described his "seedling moment" of becoming a plant person as a confluence of regional, personal, and cultural history:

> We were assigned a project to do a traditional Ojibwe activity by my professor Pebaamibines, Dennis Jones. And he was just like do Ojibwe activity, write a paper about it. So I went to sugar bush, *iskigamizigan*. And, we, I went to Porky White's Sugar Bush in Independence, Minnesota, and we made syrup and I saw garlic mustard for the first time under the snow. And I was just like, this is amazing. I don't even know if I could have told you at the time why it was amazing, but it just felt amazing. You know, I think I was already getting that sense of, nature is uncontrollable, nature also has no opinions of me. And I think that was what I was like needing at the time. . . When that assignment was assigned,

> I had just found out my father was dead. He had died four months before and I had just found out, like on Facebook or something like that, which it was really a coincidence 'cause I mean, the man had lived that long and right when I started wondering about him, he dies. Right. So it was interesting timing. And so I really was look, you know, I would never have that closure as a man getting nothing from my father all my life and then having that kind of that book shut. And so I would never get it and, and nature seemed like . . . nature just seemed like it had what I needed. (Clemens 2022)

Clemens took direction from this moment and has gone on to build a life around foraging, sharing the importance of eating wild food and medicines. He links these ideas to the importance of tending the land and experiencing the environment. Together, these form a synergistic process of being and staying well while reckoning with challenging issues in contemporary society, like poverty, racism, and environmental destruction. Foraging has, as he said, given his life "a yes" (Clemens 2022).

Storytelling and Story-listening

Tending relationships that touch both nature and history is a strategy that these Plant/People participants insist is critical for health that extends beyond the physical body to sustain healthy communities and cultures. These oral histories help us perceive the tenacity of changing plant-related health practices, and how these relationships have been integral to the ways diverse people have created and continue to create the worlds in which they want to live. Sara Axtell, an anti-racist culture worker, spoke to us about her experience with learning to grow, process, and spin flax, important tasks in her ancestral heritage, with other members of her community:

> You work together on trying something and it sparks these other questions and curiosities, and then you try to follow those threads and . . . you try to weave those things back into your life. . . . We know that there's so much in . . . our culture and . . . the legacies we have from our ancestors that need healing, that need to be healed, that need to be reckoned with. And I think what we've also learned . . . is some of the remedies for that, some of the medicines [we need] . . . are in our own history. (Axtell 2022)

Turning to land and plants alongside storytelling like Axtell was doing with her flax experiments is a strategy that most Plant/People participants explicitly identify as a mode of dealing with challenging histories. Some, like Axtell, insist on the importance of storytelling and connection with land and plants in order to reckon with a painful deep past. Völva Kari Tauring, a teacher to both Bergeron and Headington, taught us about the concept of *öorlog*, a Norse word "that means the historical precedence of your existence . . . the past is seen [as] an active principle of our accumulated actions and the actions of our ancestors" (Tauring 2022). Tauring went on to explain öorlog further using a drop spindle as a metaphor:

> [There is] everything that's already been spun before us and some of that stuff is, might not be that nice. . . . There's traumas, there's alcoholism, and there's kinds of abuses, there's . . . colonization and settler debt and öorlog within there . . . you can't unspin what has been spun before you, but you can, and *should* take a look at what's in there and make some choices about which patterns you're gonna repeat and what patterns you're gonna let go of. And so, as you're drafting out the "should" that's in front of [you], you're gonna wanna get the rove smoothed out and thinned before you let go here, or it's gonna *brrp* bundle up and be just a mess. And then your descendants are gonna have to figure out what to do with that. . . . So if you take your time

in the moment and pull the "shoulds" that are in front of you smooth, then you can let go of that moment and then it spins up. The past spins up to meet you. You don't ever have to think about what's out here [gesturing at the wool roving about to be spun] as much as what's in the past. (Tauring 2022)

Working through historical challenges experienced or wrought by ancestors via storytelling and land- and plant-based ritual is fundamental to the work that people like Bergeron and Tauring bring to their herbal and cultural practices. The place of plants and stories as partners during challenges extends beyond deeper histories and, as many participants articulated, has been critical in surviving and growing in deeply difficult moments. Tauring told us about her experiences with flowers in her yard during the weeks and months following George Floyd's murder in May 2020 when Minneapolis and St. Paul experienced an uprising demanding racial justice and systemic change in our cities:

> The plants came up to support me and the flowers were, so—there were so many flowers that whole summer—flowers came up that I'd never, never seen before in the garden. . . Wednesdays were called Weeping Wednesdays that whole summer, and I'd fill the kiddie pool up with water, and then I'd put all the flowers in and then I would just cry and cry and cry as much as I had to just to get all the sadness out and then water just would go over all the plants and they would bloom again and again, and again. Plants bloomed longer that year than ever. Like plants bloomed and bloomed and bloomed way past their usual end time that whole summer. . . . . It was really, really, very, very kind. Nature knows when we're in pain. (Tauring 2022)

Tauring touched on the resilience that relationships with plants and land can breed in the face of devastating cultural moments.

Reishi Leaf is an herbalist, therapist, and herbal medic who has been active in land protection spaces (Leaf 2022). They spoke to the importance of storytelling as a way of building connections especially in challenging spaces and moments:

> Something ... that I think is important to say is just, telling some of these stories and talking about care and connection to plants and connection to land, especially in political campaigns, I think is really important for our learning and for posterity and for healing even. And there's a very real element of security culture and ... that's a line that I'm trying to find right now, is how do we share stories that are worth telling and worth remembering and worth learning from. And also how they fit into this larger project of connection. And then also how to maintain the privacy and the necessary security because the reality is these kinds of political movements are extremely targeted by the state. (Leaf 2022)

Being in places of political action can be traumatizing for protesters, and herbal medic work felt like creating a space for healing trauma. For Leaf, talking with activists in their medic tent and offering them herbal teas and other remedies was an important way of supporting community health in extraordinarily stressful situations. Telling their stories to us was a complex decision, and Leaf weighed the importance of having those stories heard against the risk of having them recorded. Insisting on the value of plant and land relationships in a public space like a freely available oral history interview that marked Leaf's ideas and experiences was also a political action toward healing in and of itself (Leaf 2022).

Conclusion

The thought community that participants in Plant/People represent has redefined how we understand the history of medicine in this region. They demonstrate some of the ways that plants, land, storytelling, and history are deeply intertwined with both personal and community health and healing. These herbalists, activists, gardeners, culture workers, and other plant people insist that relations with plants and land *are* health. These interviews have also shifted how we think about the purposes of research on the history of medicine. Participants who are cultural elders have insisted that we recognize ourselves as part of this research and fully engage in our own self-study in order to be responsible members of this community. We are certainly students as we begin to work through understanding the ways that we as members of the academic community have our own öorlog to understand as we spin new work that should do better than what we have done before.

References

Armbrecht, Ann. 2021. *The Business of Botanicals*. White River Junction, VT: Chelsea Green.

Axtell, Sara. 2022. Interview by Macey Flood and Emily Beck, August 12.

Bergeron, Cheré. 2022. Interview by Macey Flood and Emily Beck, March 8.

Cameron, Catherine M., Paul Kelton, and Alan C. Swedlund, eds. 2015. *Beyond Germs: Native Depopulation in North America*. Tucson, AZ: University of Arizona Press.

Clemens, Tim. 2022. Interview by Macey Flood and Emily Beck, April 25.

Dougherty, Anne Kathleen. 2005. *Herbal Voices: American Herbalism through the Words of American Herbalists*. New York, NY: Psychology Press.

Fett, Sharla M. 2002. *Working Cures: Healing, Health, and Power on Southern Slave Plantations*. Chapel Hill, NC: University of North Carolina Press.

Flannery, Michael A., and Alex Berman. 2001. *America's Botanico-Medical Movements: Vox Populi*. London: Pharmaceutical Products Press.

Flood, Macey, and Emily Beck. 2024. "Plant/People." *Plant/People*. Last updated January 1, 2024. z.umn.edu/plantpeople.

Flood, Macey, and Natasha Myhal. 2022. "White Pine in Time and Place: Anishinaabe History, Western Herbalism, and the Settler Dynamics of Appropriation." *History of Pharmacy and Pharmaceuticals* 63 (2): 302–27.

Gabriel, Joseph. 2019. "Indian Secrets, Indian Cures, and the Early History of the United States Pharmacopoeia." In Matthew Crawford and Joseph Gabriel, eds., *Drugs on the Page: Pharmacopoeias and Healing Knowledge in the Early Modern Atlantic World*. Pittsburgh, PA: University of Pittsburgh Press. 240–262.

Geniusz, Mary Siisip. 2015. *Plants Have So Much to Give Us, All We Have to Do Is Ask: Anishinaabe Botanical Teachings*. Minneapolis, MN: University of Minnesota Press.

Griggs, Barbara [Barbara Van der Zee]. 1997. *Green Pharmacy: The History and Evolution of Western Herbal Medicine*. Rochester, VT: Inner Traditions/Bear.

Headington, Donyelle. 2022. Interview by Macey Flood and Emily Beck, August 11.

Horn, Gavin Van, Robin Wall Kimmerer, and John Hausdoerffer, eds. 2021. *Kinship: Belonging in a World of Relations*. Vol. 1–5. Libertyville, IL: Humans and Nature Press Books.

Kimmerer, Robin Wall. 2013. *Braiding Sweetgrass: Indigenous Wisdom, Scientific Knowledge and the Teachings of Plants*. Minneapolis, MN: Milkweed Editions.

Leaf, Reishi. 2022. Interview by Macey Flood and Emily Beck, November 11.

Philpott, Jane, and John K. Crellin. 1990. *Trying to Give Ease: Tommie Bass and the Story of Herbal Medicine*. Durham, NC: Duke University Press.

Raadt, LuAnn. 2022. Interview by Macey Flood and Emily Beck, April 1, transcript, Plant/People Oral History Collection, 35.

Schiebinger, Londa. 2007. *Plants and Empire: Colonial Bioprospecting in the Atlantic World*. Cambridge, MA: Harvard University Press.

Simpson, Leanne Betasamosake. 2011. *Dancing on Our Turtle's Back: Stories of Nishnaabeg Re-creation, Resurgence and a New Emergence*. Winnipeg: Arbeiter Ring Publishing.

Tauring, Kari. 2022. Interview by Macey Flood and Emily Beck, April 1.

Whorton, James C. 2002. *Nature Cures: The History of Alternative Medicine in America*. Oxford: Oxford University Press.

Wisecup, Kelly. 2013. *Medical Encounters: Knowledge and Identity in Early American Literatures*. Amherst, MA: University of Massachusetts Press.

8. Making Vulnerable

Exposure to Harm of Institutionalized Older Adults in Lima, Peru

MAGDALENA ZEGARRA CHIAPPORI

Early one morning, as soon as I arrived at La Merced, the shelter for abandoned older adults where I was undertaking dissertation fieldwork, I looked for Gerardo, so I could accompany him to the center's medical unit. Gerardo was eighty-one years old, extremely thin, and used a dilapidated wheelchair to get around. That morning I offered to take him to the medical unit, a small facility within the center where older adults would go if they had any health problems. Gerardo had been suffering from respiratory problems. When we arrived at the unit, all the doors to the consulting rooms were closed. I knocked on each one of them, but nobody opened. Gerardo suggested that we wait for a staff member to arrive. After twenty minutes of waiting, a nursing technician appeared. I approached her hurriedly and explained Gerardo's situation. But the technician showed little concern and told me: "A nurse is sure to come and see you. I have other things to do. This is normal in winter. Many residents have respiratory problems. Someone will come to deal with you." After making this dismissive statement, the technician withdrew, having offered us no help.

Gerardo said to me, "They don't care about us. If you die, it's better for them. One less to deal with." I was shocked by his words. But Gerardo had to see a doctor, so we continued to wait. In the hour that followed, more staff arrived at the unit. I addressed each of the nurses, doctors, and nursing technicians, but, one by one, they ignored us. Their excuses were many and varied: "This gentleman is not among the patients I have to see today"; "I am not on duty in this unit, you will have to wait for the doctor to come at 3 p.m."; or "Miss, this man is not my priority, I am responsible for the patients in pavilion four." One nurse even suggested that Gerardo's fragile condition was his own fault: "He is in the dependents' ward. He leaves his room to go to the patio. He shouldn't go out. He's exposed himself to the air and now he is sick. This gentleman is irresponsible, and he gives us more work than we already have." From my perspective, the staff members' excuses were unacceptable. Prostrate in his chair, skinny and fragile, Gerardo was experiencing discomfort and urgently needed care. The fact that he needed someone to provide immediate medical attention left him in a situation of extreme vulnerability. In his current state, he was dependent on others to provide him with assistance so that he could recover his health and thus begin to feel better. But needing care, in this case, was not enough for those with medical expertise to take action. He was dismissed and ignored by each staff member, and Gerardo's life was in danger as long as the help he required was not provided.

In this chapter, I argue that needing and providing care places many men and women in this nursing home in a situation of extreme vulnerability. In this context, being an older adult who experiences vulnerability means being exposed to circumstances in which lives are placed at risk, existence is insecure, and individuals find themselves at the mercy of medical staff—who are themselves exploited in their workplace—who dismiss their bodily conditions, fail to value their lives, and delay their medical needs. People like Gerardo are deprived of protection and rights, and excluded from decision-making regarding their illnesses and well-being. Older adults denied care or provided with care that worsens their conditions become vulnerable in the same way that medical workers at the facility—men and women from the lower socioeconomic sectors of the capital city—receive precarious salaries and are workwise invisible to La Merced's administration. In the context of the institution that is the subject of this study, being vulnerable means being exposed to harm, and unfortunately, in many cases, these individuals—both institutional residents and staff—are physically, morally, or psychologically damaged.

This chapter begins with a detailed description of the institution, its precarious aspects, and its failings. A discussion follows exploring recent debates in social sciences with regard to the concept of vulnerability. The chapter ends with ethnographic material from the field demonstrating that, for these residents, needing care has as its corollary that their lives are not apprehended as valuable or that, in the words of Judith Butler, they are "ungrievable" (Butler 2009).

Growing Old in La Merced

La Merced, the shelter providing care to Gerardo, is one of forty-six accredited elderly residential care centers by the Ministry of Women and Vulnerable Populations. The Law for the Elderly defines a residential care center as a public or private facility space accredited by the State where comprehensive and specialized care services are provided for older adults. At the time of my fieldwork (2017–2019), the institution housed approximately 335 elderly adults who came from the poorest sectors of the city. La Merced is, therefore, the largest facility in Peru providing assistance to men and women experiencing economic deprivation and social risk in old age.

Lacking the financial resources to provide appropriate care to its residents, La Merced shelter is only one of several decrepit facilities throughout Peru where people socially vanish as a result of severed kin ties and inadequate institutional assistance. At La Merced, destitution, oblivion, and postponement weigh heavily on people's everyday lives. The deprivation, isolation, and mistreatment are evident when encountering the stale smell of an overcrowded medical unit or when touching and looking at the dirty walls, damaged and permeated by humidity. In this shelter, older adults who lack family networks, care, and economic security are falling through the cracks of a precarious health infrastructure that obliterates them and their well-being.

The material and emotional environment of this shelter, with its deprivations and absences, demonstrates the precarious position these older adults occupy not only in the institution, but across the socioeconomic landscape of the nation. According to the most recent count completed by the Peruvian National Institute of Statistics in 2020, more than 3.7 million persons aged sixty years and older live in Peru (Instituto Nacional de Estadística e Informática 2020). Due to the unprecedented aging of Peru's population, concern for older adults is an emerging social issue. Nevertheless, the efforts to offer appropriate services to this group are enormously deficient. People in Peru are living longer (as in the rest of the world), but the conditions remain very precarious. In La Merced, providing older adults with appropriate care is compromised by weak public policies; staff exploitation; inadequate funding; institutional corruption; and, most recently, of course, COVID-19.

Nurse technicians and nurses, almost all women, are the main care providers at La Merced. The staff range across ages from their twenties to sixties, and their experience at La Merced varies considerably. The majority graduated from nursing schools whose programs, quite often, did not meet the standards of the National Superintendence of Higher University Education, the Peruvian public entity responsible for securing the quality of accreditation of higher educational institutions. With a poor education and exploited by La Merced, these women occupied a precarious economic situation due to low salary as well as other factors. Most of these women also came from the lower socioeconomic sectors of the capital city. Most were single mothers or daughters who had to look after their own parents or grandparents. As many of them told me, these conditions made them feel exploited by the institution. Underpaid, exhausted, lacking necessary resources to provide appropriate care, and often feeling abused—they had the most demanding job and received the lowest salary—many of these women delivered assistance to residents, sometimes in neglectful and uncompassionate ways.

In general, Peruvians tend to age at home with their families, who become the main care providers. This is seen as the ideal way to grow old. Institutionalized aging is not the custom in Peru, but today, many families face the challenges resulting from a predatory neoliberalist dynamic that strips them from financial security, free time, and other resources, leaving them with no choice other than to send their relatives to places like La Merced. As a result, care homes for the elderly in Peru are emerging as increasingly common options where people grow old and, eventually, die. For the people with whom I spoke, however, institutionalized life was difficult. Severed kin ties and poor institutional assistance makes La Merced emblematic of "zones of social abandonment": ambiguous places where people are caught between memory and nonmemory, existence and absence, life and death (Biehl 2005).

Vulnerability: What Does It Mean?

Vulnerability has come to the fore in scholarly discourse as a consequence of greater popular awareness of susceptibility to violence, injury, insecurity, and instability (Gilson 2020). In the social sciences, vulnerability is defined as the degree to which a system is susceptible to and is unable to cope with adverse effects; its key parameters are the stress to which a system is exposed, its sensitivity, and its adaptive capacity. Vulnerability is driven by inadvertent or deliberate human action that reinforces self-interest and the distribution of power (Adger 2006). In this sense, who is vulnerable has to do with who holds power and how power is distributed. More broadly, this attention to how vulnerability is produced and managed leads to the conclusion that vulnerability is the effect of social power (Butler, Gambetti, and Sabsay 2016).

In popular and policy discourses, vulnerability is consistently depicted as an affliction pertaining solely to underprivileged, oppressed, or marginalized members of society (Browne, Danely, and Rosenow 2020). But treating the problem of vulnerability as a problem that is simply given (the vulnerable are the problem) shifts attention away from the sociopolitical structures and cultural imaginaries that create, exacerbate, or perpetuate harm and suffering in the first place. The politicization of vulnerability requires a thoroughgoing consideration of social, economic, and historical structures of oppression and injustice, which determine the discourses of vulnerability and render certain populations more vulnerable than others through the unequal distribution of risk and harm as well as the unequal distribution of quality of care. The truth is that certain groups have been rendered as vulnerable, precarious, or abject by the forces of global neoliberal capitalism. The concept of structural vulnerability highlights the pathways through which specific local hierarchies and broader sets of power relations may exacerbate an individual's proneness to danger, insecurity, and injury (Bourgois et al. 2017).

Recognizing that socioeconomic and demographic attributes place individuals in a hierarchical social order that constrains their ability to access well-being leads to a broader understanding that vulnerability is a universally shared condition. Butler understands the term as a feature of embodied relations as she situates vulnerability within a social ontology that proposes that bodies are always produced and mediated within the fabrics of social life and subjected to the latter's "operations of power" (Butler, Gambetti, and Sabsay 2016, 1). Being vulnerable, hence, is the condition under which one's life is always in some sense in the hands of the other (Butler 2009, 14). According to Butler, as cited in Gilson, vulnerability is understood as a corporeal affectivity and a formative relationality and "thus as the basis for becoming the subjects that we are. . . . Vulnerability is a constant, ineradicable aspect of being a finite, embodied, social being" (Gilson 2020, 89). Butler states that "each body is straightaway given over to someone else, and its livability depends on whether the condition of shared bodily vulnerability leads to care or exploitation" (cited in Browne, Danely, and Rosenow 2020, 17).

Butler's argument that vulnerability emerges as part of social relations directs us to ask how vulnerability ought to be understood as relational and social and, at the same time, always appearing in the context of specific social and historical relations that may be analyzed concretely (Butler, Gambetti, and Sabsay 2016, 4). Recognizing vulnerability as a universal condition of dependency, relationality, or corporeal affectivity also requires recognizing it as situational, realized and experienced differentially (Gilson 2020, 88).

This chapter explores the relational process that places the older adults of this center in conditions of vulnerability as their fragile lives depend on the care and attention provided by medical staff who are themselves extremely exhausted and disempowered. Elderly residents experiencing physical and cognitive decline lack resistance strategies and thus are at the mercy of those who care for them or, in many cases, neglect them. This analysis explores the power that caregivers wield over their patients, for better or worse. Yet this analysis argues that vulnerability is more complicated than what occurs on an individual level. These older adults are made vulnerable because they are trapped in a precarious and decrepit structure—the nursing home care system—that constrains their prospects for well-being. In other words, their position in the hierarchical social order in which they are embedded limits almost all aspects of their lives, transgresses their bodies, and trespasses against their human dignity.

Making Vulnerable

An emerging body of scholarship in the field of gerontology has addressed the tendency to understand this stage primarily as negative, hopeless, or deteriorating (Havighurst 1961; Rowe and

Kahn 1997). Proponents of neoliberal ideals such as individual freedom, self-governance, and productivity have promoted the idea that aging should be successful, active, and healthy. On the surface, this aging model is highly appealing and inspiring. Older citizens do not want to be burdens. What could be more empowering for the elderly than to lead an old age in which they can eradicate the declines, vulnerabilities, and dependencies of living too long? However, critics of this aging model argue that we live today in a society where successful aging is a contemporary obsession (Lamb 2017; Taylor 2017; Leibing 2017). As a consequence, those who can fend for themselves live fulfilling, productive, and healthy lives, while those who "cannot succeed in avoiding oldness are liable to experience blame and social exclusion" (Lamb, Robbins-Ruszkowski, and Corwin 2017).

The subjects of this research project, older men and women living in La Merced, are in positions of acute vulnerability and cannot put up any kind of resistance due to their advanced level of physical and cognitive decline. Some individuals suffer from Alzheimer's disease and are unable to retain day-to-day memories or their personal histories. Others are bedridden and spend hours tied by their arms and legs to their beds to prevent them from falling or wandering around. Some residents are incapable of speech or movement and are therefore unable to object if their bodies or rights are violated. The people I write about here are powerless, live at risk of harm, and are short of protection. Their vulnerability lies in the fact that they are dependent upon the good will and expert assistance provided by others, including caregivers and institution staff. In an institution as precarious as La Merced, where staff are underpaid and exploited, and where care infrastructures are falling apart, the probability of caregivers providing medical assistance respecting older adults' bodies, wishes, and needs is really very small.

Care is often invoked as a straightforward corollary to vulnerability, whether in the form of "self care" or care for others (Browne, Danely, and Rosenow 2020). Hence, the relationship between vulnerability and care might seem to be complementary and harmonious: vulnerability requires care and care alleviates vulnerability. Yet vulnerability often elicits responses of aggression, revulsion, or attack rather than care. Care can manifest in highly ambiguous and contradictory ways, and in many contexts is intimately interwoven with coercion, exploitation, and exclusion. These tensions between care and vulnerability are explored in the ethnographic vignettes that follow. These stories reveal that care provided to the residents of this center is highly contested because it violates their persons, including their bodies and their dignity. Care that causes the subjugation of the person, the annulment of the body, and the denial of the dignity of residents transforms them into liminal entities, situated between the living and the dead, the human and the nonhuman, those arousing pity and the abject. The mere recognition of the vulnerability of these older adults does not, in the majority of cases, compel an "ethical response" from staff and caregivers (Gilson 2020, 86).

Saturnino

I first met Saturnino when I helped staff members to adjust the position of a bedridden resident. I met Saturnino a second time when the staff asked me to feed him, as the institution was short of staff and time was in equally short supply. As he ate the spoonfuls of food, I noticed that his wrists were tied to the bed with cloth ropes that restrained him from moving. Later that day, I asked a nursing technician why Saturnino was tied to the bed. She said it was a security measure; otherwise, he might fall from the bed, rip out his Foley catheter, or handle his own feces. The woman finished her explanation with conviction: "It is for his own good. I have to take care of him."

A few days later, I decided to spend the morning with Saturnino. He hardly spoke anymore and welcomed me by raising and waving his right hand—as far as he was able, since cloth ropes were used to restrain him. This gesture was performed weakly, with little physical strength and energy. I held his hand in mine and could see that the cloth ropes were leaving bruises on his wrists. I looked into his eyes and he looked back at me sadly, or so it seemed to me. I spoke into his ear because Saturnino could barely hear: "Does it hurt?" He responded in a very weak voice, breathing heavily: "Yes."

I also noticed that there was a bad smell in the room. I realized that Saturnino's diaper needed changing, and that his feces had stained the bed sheets. I left his room to look for the nursing technician, so that Saturnino could be cleaned up. When I found her, I told her that Saturnino urgently needed a clean diaper. She replied, "At noon the other shift comes on duty. They will change it." I insisted, "But, Miss, the sheets are stained. Noon is still an hour away." The nursing technician, disturbed by my insistence, raised her voice and said, "I can't now. The next shift will change him. Don't insist, Miss." I went back to the room and whispered to Saturnino that I had failed in my attempt to bring a nursing technician to change his diaper. His features expressed his resignation and he asked me to draw closer. He spoke in my ear again with that faint voice and told me very slowly, taking a breath between each word (talking too much exhausted him); "It's OK."

Noon came and nobody from the next shift came to change Saturnino's diaper. We waited for so long that lunch arrived. I helped him to eat his smoothie and purple corn dessert. The fetid odor, however, was all-pervasive. It was three o'clock before a nursing technician finally entered the room. The only bed was Saturnino's. She was taking each bedridden patient's pulse, and it was Saturnino's turn. The technician crossed the threshold of the room and exclaimed, "What a smell! How he smells! Haven't they changed him? He's filthy!" "No," I answered her. "We have been waiting since 11 a.m." It seemed to me that the nursing technician reacted with compassion, and she proceeded to change Saturino's diaper and sheets. Finally, he was clean, but it had taken an infuriatingly long time for him to be seen by the staff.

Manuel

Manuel was a very cheerful resident. Within the institution, he was classified as a psychiatric patient and prescribed psychotropic medication. But the way in which he was "labeled" within the institution did not prevent him from behaving with the energy of a child: he liked to sing, paint, and run through the corridors of the shelter. He used to wake up very early; I always saw him when I entered the center in the mornings.

My time at La Merced only involved spending time with the residents. The director of the center did not give me permission to participate in the multidisciplinary team meetings, where she, along with other professionals such as psychologists, social workers, and doctors, met to discuss patients in a declining state of health. Although I did not attend the meetings, I had made friends with two workers at the center—Alexia and Carmen—and sometimes they told me what was discussed in the meetings. Days went by, and I noticed that I no longer saw Manuel when I arrived at the institution. Around five days passed, and I didn't see him.

Thursday came, which was the day our schedules coincide, and Alexia, Carmen, and I went to have lunch at a nearby restaurant. I asked them if they knew anything about Manuel, because I hadn't seen him in the past few days. Alexia answered, "They screwed up." "What?" I asked. Carmen continued with the story: "At the last meeting of the multidisciplinary team, the director said that the nurses in the psychiatric ward mixed up the medicines and gave some patients the wrong medication. Manuel was one of them. He's been doped up for the past few days. That's why you haven't seen him." Alexia continued, "The director didn't seem to think this was too serious, though. She even said 'certain psychiatric patients who are very active and energetic have to be drugged. That way, when not bothered by them, the nursing technicians will be able to work better.'"

As I continued my research over several weeks, I did not see several of the psychiatric patients whom I had previously seen quite frequently. I don't know if the doping measure suggested by the director had been applied or if, yet again, the nurses had made mistakes with the distribution of psychotropic medication to the residents.

Marisol

Night was falling at the shelter and it was dinnertime. Marisol, the nursing technician responsible for the ten bedridden residents on wing 10, seemed rather distressed. I was sitting with Jaime, one of the residents, in his room. We were talking about the political situation in Peru when trays of food arrived from the kitchen. I left Jaime and went to offer Marisol some help feeding the residents. "Thank you very much," she told me. "If you don't help me I'll never finish. My colleague was sent to the hospital today and I've been left alone. You know how it is here, nobody can cope with it." I took a tray into another room. While I fed the lumpy, blended shake to a resident, I could hear Marisol admonish one of the residents she was feeding. "Hurry up, I don't have all night. Swallow faster. I still have nine more to feed. If you don't hurry, I'll leave you without eating and go to another room."

I let a moment pass after hearing those words and went out into the central hall of the wing. Marisol had finished with the resident she had admonished, and now she was feeding a woman in a wheelchair. However, the way she was doing it shocked me. Marisol was pouring the mixture into the woman's mouth from a pitcher. This technique allowed her to work so quickly: the resident barely had time to swallow the food, and from time to time she regurgitated what she had swallowed.

A few days later, Marisol and I met again in the wing. It was morning and Marisol had to bathe some of the residents. Just as she was preparing to start with the first resident, the supervising nurse arrived. She pulled Marisol towards the hall and began to rebuke her. I could hear everything because I was also in the hall, folding clothes from the laundry. "You are too slow. Reports indicate that everything is taking you longer than it should. Last week those in the kitchen complained that your residents' food containers arrived too late, and the cooks had to stay up late washing everything." Marisol replied that her coworker was absent because she had been sent to the hospital and she had to manage on her own the needs of the ten bedridden residents on wing 10. "That's none of my concern," the supervising nurse told her. "You know how things are here. If you're not going to keep up, you'll have to leave. We are understaffed, and, on top of that, you're always behind with your work. You've been warned—if it happens again, I'll talk to the director and have you removed."

Conclusion

These three vignettes reflect how care and vulnerability are affected by power and how vulnerability will depend on how people participate in the distribution and management of power—and, in the case of the residents of La Merced, if they are abused as a result. In other words, in a context such as in La Merced, being vulnerable has to do with the degree to which residents are injurable, susceptible to harm, and deprived of their humanity. Who has power in these scenarios? At first glance, the institution's staff have power over the residents, as long as they have the ability to decide when to change a diaper, how to feed, how to administer medication, or how to tie up or drug residents deemed to be a "nuisance." Often, staff approach residents' bodies with little gentleness, such as when dressing or bathing them. Other times, they talk to them harshly—for example, if a resident was eating slowly and the nurse technician had to feed other residents with the clock running against her. There were instances in which I was able to verify that the medical team did offer care to the residents in a delicate and respectful manner. However, in most cases, I witnessed how residents of La Merced—their persons, their dignity, and their bodies—were transgressed. The medical staff make residents vulnerable because they exercise unequal and disproportionate control over them.

The third vignette, however, highlights Butler's affirmation that all of us are, to some degree, at the mercy of others. It is not just residents who find themselves in a situation of vulnerability—their lives at risk, exposed to mistreatment, or subject to abuse. Marisol, the nursing technician who treated her patients harshly, also found herself in a vulnerable position with regard to supervisors who wielded more power and claimed more seniority in the hierarchy. While Marisol did, in some ways, abuse the residents, she also experienced abuse from officials higher up than her. In a setting where care was precariously provided due to a lack of resources and staff, both the most fragile residents and the least important employees found themselves in an environment of risk in which, to differing degrees, they lacked power.

During her shifts, Marisol found herself constantly trying to sustain herself in an environment where she experienced job insecurity and an eroded sense of well-being. The social position that Marisol experienced in this shelter for the old was between *being* vulnerable and *making* vulnerable. In the end, both residents and nursing technicians, as well as nurses and doctors, are embedded in a hierarchical structure of power and unequal relationships of dependency (Browne, Danely, and Rosenow 2020). Each group of individuals is exposed to harm, open to being wounded, and susceptible to exploitation, from the resident whose wrists are tied and covered in bruises to the nursing technician who is intimidated by the threat of losing their job if unable to maintain the rhythm of the daily routine.

For many of the older adults with whom I spoke, growing old in La Merced meant they lacked the power to name and claim. Struggling to endure in a place they tended to refer to as "hopeless" and "demeaning," these people's lives resemble what Giorgio Agamben (1998) has called "bare life": life divested of social recognition, affection, well-being, and even rights. For older adults, this means being *vulnerable* in *this* context. Under this care-neglect logic, residents are no longer seen as people; instead, these individuals are viewed as something other than human, even as objects. They are considered, above all else, as bothersome or, even worse, as injurable, treated as inert and disposable bodily matter (Tzelepis 2016). I believe that when an individual is left on sheets stained with excrement or tied to their bed with cloth ropes that cause injury, they cease to be seen as a person with dignity and agency, deserving of respect. Because of the treatment they receive, the residents of this center have become things or, perhaps, just bodies—things or bodies seen as being in the way; things or bodies that nobody wants to deal with; things or bodies that nobody wants to take responsibility for, that are best annulled. The bodies of older adults cannot be dissociated from infrastructural and environmental conditions in which they live (Butler 2016, 19). According to Achille Mbembe (2019), the vulnerability to which these people are exposed is a form of necropolitics: institutionalized violence that renders residents—those in need of care and protection—as disposable entities, subjects who, in the best-case scenario, receive biopolitical care but are dismissed as persons desirous of a better, livable life.

These residents are men and women who have been forced to survive all their lives without formal work, without a family to support them, without access to quality education, and without health insurance. They are destined, even doomed, to end their days in a total institution, which, although it offers them a refuge from the harshness of life on the street, does not provide care that recognizes them as individuals with rights or offer them an autonomous, dignified, or even hopeful way of living. A cartography of those who reside in this space and under these forms of care reveals that those who live here have always been on the margins; they are the vulnerable whose lives are the most difficult to live.

Being vulnerable in La Merced, means, in Butler's words, living an "ungrievable" life, as these lives are always in the hands of others; an ungrievable life is "one that cannot be mourned because it has never been lived; that is, it has never counted as a life at all" (Butler 2009, 38).

The lives of these residents do not fully qualify as lives "or are, from the start, not conceived as lives within certain epistemological frames" (Butler 2009, 1). The lives of many of these residents—and of some staff members too—are vulnerable and ungrievable because the mechanisms of power push them towards the margins; they are invisible, their suffering is silenced, and their bodies are trespassed. These residents are vulnerable because they are individuals who possess a life—a *biological* life—but, because of the limited amount of agency they exercise (due to physical or cognitive impairment), they are not apprehended by the staff or even by society as intelligible actors whose lives have value. Instead, they are systematically neglected to the point that their comfort, their well-being, and their quality of life are deemed irrelevant by those around them. Being vulnerable in La Merced means that an individual's life does not matter, that it is irrelevant.

The ways in which people grow old and die say a lot about our societies. I believe the time has come to address experiences of old age that, like those of many residents at this center, are unlivable, whether due to being socially neglected, suffering pain, or experiencing fragility. These are, of course, challenging stories to listen to, to witness, to engage with. These stories are also challenging because they both confirm the obstacles and demands facing vulnerable populations, including patients and staff, as well as the dilemmas posed by a research method that approaches stories seriously and with compassion. In our societies—societies where care is more uncertain and unreliable—we must address these narratives in order to achieve better quality of life, not only for older adults, but for everyone who is located in a position of vulnerability. That is the challenge we, as a post COVID-19 society, must embrace: to listen attentively to the narrative of the vulnerable in order to set into motion public policies, national and international strategies, and health protocols that can allow us to live in a better world.

Aging actively and healthily is, without a doubt, the desired outcome, but not all of us will achieve this. How will these people age, these individuals whose bodies are transgressed and cannot put up any kind of resistance against abuse, due to their physical and cognitive decline? How should old age be addressed among those who are vulnerable, at risk, or in danger? I believe that, in these times, it is imperative that we think about the development of life strategies that will make it possible to age with dignity and well-being, free from harm, including in the cases of those who are most vulnerable. We need to open ourselves up to a new way of rethinking vulnerability, thereby ending mistreatment, aggression, or abuse and thinking of vulnerability as a condition that predisposes us to care, to provide human warmth, to offer respect and the possibility of leading a life that it is possible to live, by appealing to those on the other side of vulnerability—if anyone can ever truly escape this condition—to look at those who are vulnerable as fellow human beings. The vulnerability of the other should challenge us to treat them as a human being just like us, with the same freedoms, rights, and values. Being open to listening to the challenging stories of people who live under these dire circumstances is the first step of many toward building a more compassionate society, where no one is left behind.

References

Adger, Neil. 2006. "Vulnerability." *Global Environmental Change* 16 (Winter): 268–81.

Agamben, Giorgio. 1998. *Homo Sacer: Sovereign Power and Bare Life.* Stanford, CA: Stanford University Press.

Biehl, Joao. 2005. *Vita: Life in a Zone of Social Abandonment.* Berkeley, CA: University of California Press.

Bourgois, Philippe, Seth M. Holmes, Kim Sue, and James Quesada. 2017. "Structural Vulnerability: Operationalizing the Concept to Address Health Disparities in Clinical Care." *Academic Medicine* 92 (3): 299–307.

Browne, Victoria, Jason Danely, and Doerthe Rosenow. 2020. "Vulnerability and the Politics of Care: Transdisciplinary Dialogues." In *Vulnerability and the Politics of Care: Transdisciplinary Dialogues*, ed. Victoria Browne, Jason Danely, and Doerthe Rosenow, 1–30. Oxford: Oxford University Press.

Butler, Judith. 2009. *Frames of War*. London: Verso.

Butler, Judith. 2016. "Rethinking Vulnerability and Resistance." In *Vulnerability in Resistance*, ed. Judith Butler, Zeynep Gambetti, Leticia Sabsay, 12–27. Durham, NC: Duke University Press.

Butler, Judith, Zeynep Gambetti, and Leticia Sabsay. 2016. "Introduction." In *Vulnerability in Resistance*, ed. Judith Butler, Zeynep Gambetti, Leticia Sabsay, 1–11. Durham, NC: Duke University Press.

Gilson, Erinn. 2020. "The Problems and Potentials of Vulnerability." In *Vulnerability and the Politics of Care: Transdisciplinary Dialogues*, ed. Victoria Browne, Jason Danely, and Doerthe Rosenow, 85–107. Oxford: Oxford University Press.

Havighurst, Robert. 1961. "Successful Aging." *Gerontologist* 1 (1): 8–13.

Instituto Nacional de Estadística e Informática (INEI). 2020. "Situación de la población adulta mayor; Trimestre: Octubre-Noviembre-Diciembre 2023." *Informe técnico* (1): 1–51.

Lamb, Sarah. 2017. *Successful Aging as a Contemporary Obsession: Global Perspectives*. New Brunswick: Rutgers University Press.

Lamb, Sarah, Jessica Robbins-Ruszkowski, and Anna Corwin. 2017. "Introduction: Successful Aging as a Twenty-First-Century Obsession." In *Successful Aging as a Contemporary Obsession: Global Perspectives*, ed. Sarah Lamb, 1–24. New Brunswick: Rutgers University Press.

Leibing, Annette. 2017. "Successful Selves? Heroic Tales of Alzheimer's Disease and Personhood in Brazil." In *Successful Aging as a Contemporary Obsession: Global Perspectives*, ed. Sarah Lamb, 203–217. New Brunswick: Rutgers University Press.

Mbembe, Achille. 2019. *Necropolitics*. Durham, NC: Duke University Press.

Rowe, John, and Robert Kahn. 1997. "Successful Aging." *Gerontologist* 37: 433–40.

Taylor, Janelle. 2017. "Should Old Acquaitance Be Forgot? Friendship in the Face of Dementia." In *Successful Aging as a Contemporary Obsession: Global Perspectives*, ed. Sarah Lamb, 126–138. New Brunswick: Rutgers University Press.

Tzelepis, Elena. 2016. "Vulnerable Corporealities and Precarious Belongings in Mona Hatoum's Art." In *Vulnerability in Resistance*, ed. Judith Butler, Zeynep Gambetti, Leticia Sabsay, 146–66. Durham, NC: Duke University Press.

Afterword

Shared Horizons: Past, Present, and Future

JEFFREY S. REZNICK AND FRANK VITALE IV

This book offers a multiplicity of challenging stories about challenging times. It is a product of a historic era and a landmark collaboration between biomedicine and the digital humanities made possible through a partnership between the National Endowment for the Humanities (NEH) and the National Library of Medicine (NLM). Indeed, this book advances the commitment of both the NEH to "expand opportunities for all Americans to participate in and benefit from humanities-centered research, education, and public programs" (NEH 2022) and the NLM to "accelerate discovery and advance health through data-driven research, reach more people in more ways through enhanced dissemination and engagement, and build a workforce for data-driven research and health" (NLM 2018b). Locating this book in the circumstances of its creation inspires us to realize a postpandemic world of increased collaboration and scholarly inquiry among even more scholars and institutions pursuing research, teaching, and learning at the intersection of biomedicine and the digital humanities. This perspective also signals that the conception, pursuit, sustainability, and impact of the medical humanities depends fundamentally on institutional culture, leadership, partnerships, and support.

"At the Interface of All Our Work . . ."

In 2012, the NEH and the NLM established a partnership to collaborate on research, education, and career initiatives located at the intersection of biomedical and humanities research (NEH

2012a; NLM 2012a). Shortly thereafter, the agencies joined with the Maryland Institute for Technology in the Humanities and Research Councils UK (now known as UK Research and Innovation) to convene the 2013 symposium *Shared Horizons: Data, Biomedicine, and the Digital Humanities* (NEH 2012b; NLM 2012b). A dozen sessions and lectures placed historians and computer scientists in conversation with biomedical researchers, librarians, and members of the public. Through sessions including "With a Wild Surmise: Intimations of Computational Biology in Keats, Carroll, and Joyce" and "Common Design Strategies for Exploring Intellectual Geographies in History and Cell Motility in Biology," *Shared Horizons* brought together disparate topics such as text mining, epidemiology, literary analysis, computer science, data analytics, and microbiology. The conference itself was relatively small: thirty-eight scholars of a variety of disciplines participated in the individual sessions, along with approximately 100 additional attendees who joined the program for the keynote address (Fraistat 2013). *Shared Horizons* might initially be mistaken as a moderate point-in-time success with little lasting impact on the long-term missions of the NEH and the NLM. To the contrary, *Shared Horizons* represented what Paul Voosen (2013) aptly described as "the beginning of a beautiful friendship," an innovative interdisciplinary partnership between the sciences and the humanities. Erez Aiden and Jean-Baptiste Michel went further, praising the conference for "betray[ing] an astonishing optimism: the idea that historians and philosophers and artists and doctors and biologists, thinking about data together, can advance their individual causes better than any of them can alone." Aiden and Michel added, "The conference title . . . was dead-on. At the interface of all our work lies the most exciting terrain in our intellectual future" (Aiden and Michel 2013, 206–7).

Examining the various research publications that have emerged from *Shared Horizons* and the NEH–NLM partnership overall, including this volume, illustrates the effectiveness and impact of both initiatives. One such article, "Gaining Insights into Epidemics by Mining Historical Newspapers," established methods for examining historical epidemiology through text mining of historical newspapers (Ewing, Ramakrishnan, and Gad 2013). The article, written by a historian and two computer scientists, appeared in the computer science journal *Computer IEEE* and has been cited in articles about medical history, computer science, data analytics, and the digital humanities (Google Scholar 2023). Interdisciplinary research such as this, involving scholars from traditionally disparate fields, points to the value of the NEH-NLM partnership as a catalyst for creating new knowledge across domains.

Notably, the NLM also contributed to the research output of *Shared Horizons* beyond published scholarship by coordinating the release of extensible markup language (XML) data from the internationally renowned IndexCat database. IndexCat is a digital resource consisting of millions of references from the printed, sixty-one-volume Index Catalogue of the Library of the Surgeon General's Office originally published from 1880 to 1961 (NLM 2013). The XML dataset describes millions of items spanning five centuries and covering a wide range of subjects such as the basic sciences, scientific research, civilian and military medicine, public health, and hospital administration (Reznick 2014). As such, the dataset is a valuable resource for medical research across disciplines. Coinciding with *Shared Horizons*, the release of this unique dataset by the NLM marked the beginning of its active engagement with a new generation of researchers. The dataset has been downloaded more than 30,000 times, demonstrating the long-term value and impact of library data curation and dissemination for researchers.

Shared Horizons therefore established the foundation for the future success of the NEH–NLM partnership (Circulating Now 2023; NEH 2018, 2020; NLM 2015, 2018a, 2020). Over the next decade, it facilitated multiple collaborations, engagements, programs, and publications involving dozens of early-career and established scholars, educators, and students in both the sciences and the humanities. These activities benefited thousands of audience members and readers, at every turn advancing the complementary missions of the agencies. Such impactful initiatives included public symposia; research workshops; cosponsored public lectures; and *Viral Networks: Connecting Digital Humanities and Medical History*, a peer-reviewed, open-access book on the digital medical humanities (Ewing and Randall 2018).

Shared Horizons . . . Worlds Apart

Shared Horizons took place in a very different time from the COVID-19 pandemic period and our post-pandemic world. The meeting was solely in-person, as scholars had been gathering at conferences for decades, and at a time when widespread video streaming of lectures was in its infancy. *Shared Horizons* also convened when online content was relatively static, well before today's pervasiveness of social media connecting users via decentralized web networks through which they access, use, and re-use their own data and the data of other users. Moreover, *Shared Horizons* marked the early period of open data policies, before the rise of critical data studies (Dalton and Thatcher 2014; boyd and Crawford 2012). Perhaps most striking of all, *Shared Horizons* occurred when scholars studied pandemic diseases uniquely through the historical record.

Little did anyone associated with *Shared Horizons* know that the future terrain Aiden and Michel anticipated would include a pandemic that would, in turn, give rise to *Data, Health, and the Digital Humanities: Shared Horizons II*, a series of virtual programs hosted by the NLM, and a scholarly book to be published by Virginia Tech Publishing—indeed the very one you are reading now—all supported by an NEH grant to Virginia Tech. Through its very character as a virtual scholarly initiative focused on studying challenging stories of the contemporary pandemic, *Shared Horizons II* reflected the hallmarks of its historic time. Each contributor brought to it not only their disciplinary perspectives but also their own experiences of lockdowns, masking, and seeing news stories in real time about pandemic-related health disparities among high-risk and underserved populations, including racial and ethnic minority groups and rural communities. Each faced social distancing combined with virtual interactions, realizing the benefits, drawbacks, and implications of both. Each witnessed the race for a vaccine, its subsequent distribution, and then the race to receive "the jab" and subsequent boosters, all while learning how to use different kinds of COVID-19 home test kits and wondering when the pandemic would become endemic.

These and related subjects—in addition to contemporary public commitments to advancing diversity, equity, and inclusion in science and society—informed the two virtual keynote lectures of *Shared Horizons II*, the first by Kim Gallon, PhD, Associate Professor of Africana Studies at Brown University, and the second by Katy Kole de Peralta, PhD, Clinical Assistant Professor of History at Arizona State University. In her lecture "Shutting the Digital Back Door: Creating Tech Justice with Health Data Liquidity and the Digital Humanities," Gallon explored the concept of the digital back door in healthcare: technological processes and tools used in healthcare, such as racially biased algorithms, infrastructural limitations, and dirty data and their historical roots in structural and systemic racism. The methodological use of the digital humanities, she argued, "offers an opportunity to eliminate digital back doors by creating more humanistic and equitable health information technology (health IT) that address health disparities and inequities" (NIH 2022a; Circulating Now 2022a). In offering her lecture "Life after Lockdown: Pandemic Perspectives from Peru," Kole de Peralta focused on *The Journal of the Plague Year: A COVID-19 Archive*, a digital, open access, crowdsourced archive. Since its inception in March 2020, she explained, its archival team has "intentionally collected pandemic stores in ethical, inclusive ways, demonstrating what we gain when we intentionally build digital humanities projects that expand beyond academic institutions and audiences." Kole de Peralta explained further that the archive "successfully partnered with universities, libraries, and contributors across the global south including the Philippines, American Samoa, India, as well as Peru" where the population experienced "one of the earliest, strictest, and longest lockdown policies, and yet it is still the global leader in COVID-19-related fatalities" (NIH 2022b; Circulating Now 2022b). Drawing on quantitative and qualitative data submitted to the archive and oral histories, Kole de Peralta examined the breaking points that undermined public health efforts and what life after lockdown looks like in Peru.

The contributors to this book attended these virtual lectures and, following each one, met virtually with the speakers for in-depth discussion and exchange of ideas about the impact of pandemic events on their research, teaching, and public service, yielding many impacts never before experienced. The groups discussed witnessing pandemic death and the disparity of public health resources in real time via media coverage. They shared their experiences of building connections with colleagues through technology while longing for renewed physical engagement and coping with isolation, even as it sometimes gave way to welcome periods of contemplation. They discussed realizing the flexibility and navigating the limits of scholarship and research in the digital space, as well as the need to be patient until circumstances could allow for renewed access to valued collections for research. Through these conversations, a distinct sense of community and camaraderie arose among *Shared Horizons II* participants. This resulting book is as much a mirror of their dialogue and witness to unprecedented times as it is a memorial of a once-in-a-lifetime event impacting human experience and health.

More Shared Horizons on the Horizon

Shared Horizons and *Shared Horizons II* bookend a decade of profound change in science and society. Time will tell whether and how the COVID-19 pandemic will accelerate this change, and how it might yield further change along with a host of other factors—from evermore data-driven research to the greater prevalence of artificial intelligence to the challenges of writing histories of the early twenty-first century based on wholly digital sources, such as blogs and social media. In all of these factors and many more, interaction between biomedicine and the digital humanities will be essential in order to navigate the challenges and opportunities of change. A particular challenge will be how to continue to meet at these intersections—intellectually, physically, and virtually—and achieve meaningful dialogue and impactful research outputs.

Born from the pandemic and reflecting its unprecedented times, this book and the partnership underpinning it represent an inspiring way forward in the postpandemic ecosystem of research and public service. Indeed, it represents part of the intellectual future that Aiden and Michel so excitedly anticipated (Aiden and Michel 2013). It should also remind readers that fruitful interactions between biomedicine and the digital humanities in this ecosystem will depend fundamentally on institutional culture, leadership, partnerships, and support. The digital medical humanities offer a unique locus of reflection so vitally needed in today's COVID-19-impacted world, where we can better understand the complex impacts of health and medicine on the human experience.

Shared Horizons has effectively characterized this intersection of human experience and health research. Looking to the future, indeed, the horizon—and with appreciation of this book and its many scholarly precedents made possible by the NEH-NLM collaboration—researchers are poised to explore many more challenging stories that will further advance our understanding of health in the diversity of spaces between data and narrative.

Note: This contribution was carried out in part by staff of the National Library of Medicine (NLM), National Institutes of Health (NIH), with support from the NLM.

References

Aiden, Erez, and Jean-Baptiste Michel. 2013. *Uncharted: Big Data as a Lens on Human Culture*. New York, NY: Riverhead Books.

boyd, danah, and Kate Crawford. 2012. "Critical Questions for Big Data." *Information, Communication & Society* 15 (5): 662–79.

Circulating Now. 2022a. "Shutting the Digital Back Door." *Circulating Now: From the Historical Collections of the National Library of Medicine* (blog), October 3.

Circulating Now. 2022b. "Life after Lockdown: Pandemic Perspectives from Peru." *Circulating Now: From the Historical Collections of the National Library of Medicine* (blog), November 3.

Circulating Now. 2023. "NLM-NEH Collaboration." *Circulating Now: From the Historical Collections of the National Library of Medicine* (blog). Accessed March 30.

Dalton, Craig, and Jim Thatcher. 2014. "What Does a Critical Data Studies Look Like and Why Do We Care?" *Society & Space*, May 12.

Ewing, E. Thomas, Naren Ramakrishnan, and Samah Gad. 2013. "Gaining Insights into Epidemics by Mining Historical Newspapers." *Computer IEEE* 46 (6): 68–72.

Ewing, E. Thomas, and Katherine Randall. 2018. *Viral Networks: Connecting Digital Humanities and Medical History*. Blacksburg, VA: Virginia Tech Publishing.

Fraistat, Neil. 2013. "Final Performance Report: Grant #HC5001512 MITH-NEH-NLM Genomics Workshop (Shared Horizons: Data, Biomedicine, and the Digital Humanities)." Grant report, August 30.

Google Scholar. 2024. Citation metrics for E. Thomas Ewing, Naren Ramakrishnan, and Samah Gad. 2013. "Gaining Insights into

Epidemics by Mining Historical Newspapers." *Computer IEEE* 46 (6): 68–73. Google. Accessed August 13, 2024.

National Endowment for the Humanities (NEH). 2012a. "NLM & National Endowment for the Humanities to Cooperate on Initiatives of Common Interest." News release, June 20.

National Endowment for the Humanities (NEH). 2012b. "NEH and Partner Organizations Co-Sponsor Symposium on Biomedicine and Digital Humanities." News release, August 6.

National Endowment for the Humanities (NEH). 2018. "NEH & NLM Renew Partnership to Collaborate on Research, Education, and Career Initiatives." News release, February 15.

National Endowment for the Humanities (NEH). 2020. "NEH & NLM Renew Partnership to Collaborate on Research, Education, and Career Initiatives." News release, December 16.

National Endowment for the Humanities (NEH). 2022. "Statement from Shelly C. Lowe on Her Confirmation as Twelfth Chair of the National Endowment for the Humanities." December 3.

National Institutes of Health (NIH). 2022a. "Shutting the Digital Back Door: Creating Tech Justice with Health Data Liquidity and the Digital Humanities." NIH VideoCasting, October 4.

National Institutes of Health (NIH). 2022b. "Life after Lockdown: Pandemic Perspectives from Peru." NIH VideoCasting, November 9.

National Library of Medicine (NLM). 2012a. "National Endowment for the Humanities and the National Library of Medicine to Partner on Research, Education, and Career Initiatives." NLM news announcement, June 20.

National Library of Medicine (NLM). 2012b. "NLM to Participate with Partners in 'Shared Horizons: Data, Biomedicine, and the Digital Humanities' Symposium." NLM news announcement, August 6.

National Library of Medicine (NLM). 2013. "NLM Releases Extensible Markup Language (XML) for IndexCat Data." NLM news announcement, April 5.

National Library of Medicine (NLM). 2015. "NEH & National Endowment for the Humanities Reaffirm Cooperation on

Initiatives of Common Interest." NLM news announcement, August 19.

National Library of Medicine (NLM). 2018a. "NEH and NLM Renew Partnership to Collaborate on Research, Education, and Career Initiatives." NLM news announcement, February 14.

National Library of Medicine (NLM). 2018b. "NLM Launches 2017–2027 Strategic Plan." NLM news announcement, March 6.

National Library of Medicine (NLM). 2020. "NLM and NEH Renew Partnership to Collaborate on Research, Education, and Career Initiatives." NLM news announcement, December 14.

Reznick, Jeffrey S. 2014. "IndexCat: Search It, Read It, Download It." *Circulating Now: From the Historical Collections of the National Library of Medicine* (blog), March 4.

Reznick, Jeffrey S., and Brett Bobley. 2016. "Synergy for the Greater Good." *Public Manager*, Association for Talent Development (blog), July 11.

Voosen, Paul. 2013. "The Beginning of a Beautiful Friendship? Biologists and Humanities Scholars Explore Digital Partnerships." *Chronicle of Higher Education* (blog), April 22.

Contributors

Emily Beck received a PhD in the history of medicine from the University of Minnesota and is the associate curator of the Wangensteen Historical Library of Biology and Medicine at the University of Minnesota. Beck's research covers multiple topics, including manuscript cultures of making in premodern Europe, human-plant relations in the contemporary midwest, and engaging health and plant humanities in innovative primary source pedagogy.

Chuan Hao (Alex) Chen completed a PhD in cultural anthropology at the University of Pennsylvania in 2023 and is in the MD/PhD program at the Perelman School of Medicine. Chen's research examines issues of race and space in relation to biosafety practices against emerging infectious diseases in the United States.

Martha L. Espinosa completed a PhD in history at Duke University (2024) and is an assistant professor of Latin American history at DePauw University. Espinosa's research focuses on the history of eugenics, contraceptive technologies, and reproductive justice in Latin America, with a focus on twentieth century Mexico.

E. Thomas Ewing completed a PhD in Russian history at the University of Michigan (1994) and is a professor of history and associate dean for research at Virginia Tech. Ewing's research explores networks of information and infection during the 1889 influenza pandemic.

Macey Flood received a PhD in the history of science, technology, and medicine from the University of Minnesota in 2021. They are an assistant professor at Metropolitan State University. Flood's research includes the reciprocity of human and environmental health, social and historical determinants of contemporary health inequities and health justice, and histories of non-biomedical health modalities in Indigenous and settler Turtle Island/North America.

Priyanka (Priya) Ganguly completed a PhD in rhetoric and writing at Virginia Tech (2023) and is an assistant professor of technical communication and rhetoric at Texas Tech University. Ganguly's research explores the issues of transnational negotiation and power and (mis)articulations in the context of global public health content creation.

Kimberly V. Jones completed a PhD at Rice University in 2023 and is currently an assistant professor of history at the University of Denver. Jones's research assesses the connections between disability, racial capitalism, and slavery in Early Republic Virginia.

Gianna May Sanchez is a PhD candidate in history at the University of Michigan and a graduate researcher at the Sterilization and Social Justice Lab. Sanchez's research focuses on the history of medicine in the twentieth century American West and within Latinx communities, with particular interest in folk healing, curanderismo, midwifery, and women's health.

Samin Rashidbeigi completed a PhD in Near Eastern studies at Princeton University in 2024 and is a postdoctoral fellow at the Medical Humanities Research Institute at Rice University. Rashidbeigi's research examines the relationships of individuals with their physical bodies through the medical technologies in the modern Middle East.

Jeffrey S. Reznick completed a PhD in modern European history at Emory University (1999) and is senior historian at the National Library of Medicine, National Institutes of Health (NIH). Reznick maintains a diverse, interdisciplinary, and highly collaborative historical research portfolio supported by the library and based on its diverse collection and associated products and services.

Frank Vitale IV completed an MLIS at the University of Wisconsin-Milwaukee (2021) and an MSc in the history of science, medicine, and technology from the University of Oxford (2018) and is assistant professor, university archivist and special collections librarian at Millersville University. Vitale's research covers multiple topics including the digital humanities, archival instruction, and the history of the Native American Boarding School Era in the American empire.

Magdalena Zegarra Chiappori received her PhD in anthropology from the University of Michigan in 2022 and is a medical anthropologist with academic interests in economies of care, old age, intimacy and affect theory, social abandonment, death, marginalized communities, and Latin American Studies. Zegarra Chiappori's research examines the life-worlds and subjective experiences of one of the most invisible, unmapped, and understudied populations of Peruvian society: the elderly urban-poor.

Made in the USA
Columbia, SC
23 October 2024